RUSSIA

AND

THE RUSSIANS.

British Library Cataloguing-in-Publication Data
A catalogue record for this book is available from
the British Library

RUSSIA AND THE RUSSIANS,

COMPRISING AN ACCOUNT OF

THE CZAR NICHOLAS

AND THE HOUSE OF ROMANOFF,

WITH A SKETCH OF

THE PROGRESS AND ENCROACHMENTS OF RUSSIA

FROM THE TIME OF THE EMPRESS CATHERINE.

By J. W. COLE, H. P. 21st Fusiliers.

> "Thrice is he arm'd that hath his quarrel just,
> And he but naked, though lock'd up in steel,
> Whose conscience with injustice is corrupted."
> SHAKESPEARE.

RUSSIA AND THE RUSSIANS.

———◆———

AFTER forty years of peace, the advent of a general war announces itself by signs and tokens which can no longer be mistaken. The enlightened nations of the world are driven into an alternative which they never desired less, and have struggled to avoid, until forbearance is construed into pusillanimity. Occupied with internal improvements and the interchange of commerce, long experience has taught them that the steam engine and the electric telegraph are more wholesome reasoners, more potent instruments of civilization and happiness, than the bayonet, the sabre, or the musquet ball. The brand of Althæa

B

is as unwelcome as mischievous, and we may hope
the fire it seeks to kindle, in this instance, will
consume, not the intended victim, but the vindictive aggressor. Those who study prophecy declare
loudly, that the fulfilment of great events foretold
in scripture, but as yet unaccomplished, is rapidly
to be expected. Many theories have been promulgated on this subject, which have excited much
interest, and would be more convincing, but that
they are sometimes contradictory and not always
intelligible. On one point only is there perfect
unanimity of opinion; namely, that Russia is to
be the prime mover, the exciting cause in the
mighty struggle about to commence; but whether
she is to issue triumphant from the trial she has
so wantonly provoked, or to be pared down from
her overweening pretensions, and restrained within
reasonable limits for the future, is another question in the argument which time only can bring
to an uncontradicted solution. As far as the doctrine of chances is open to human calculation, or
the transactions of men are regulated by human
agency; inasmuch as a good cause is preferable
to a bad one, and Providence smiles on the side
of justice, we have little to fear for the result, and
may buckle on our armour in the confidence of
victory. The ambition of the *King of the North,*
like a portentous comet " with fear of change per-

plexing nations," has long hung over us, exciting undefined terrors, and a perpetual feverish dread of ruin and combustion—the sword of Damocles for ever threatening to fall. The time appears to have arrived when the string by which it is suspended must be cut, the weapon wrested from the hands that have sharpened it, and turned in retribution on themselves. When Napoleon crossed the Niemen in 1812, with continental Europe obedient to his nod, and an invading army for which history had no parallel since the days of Xerxes, he exclaimed with oracular confidence, " Let the destinies of Russia be accomplished ! " They were, for a time (but in a manner opposite to what he had predicted), in his own discomfiture, and the annihilation of his gallant legions. Perhaps a similar impression stamped itself on the mind of Nicholas, when he ordered the passage of the Pruth, in the summer of 1853, and poured his unwelcome visitants into the defenceless Principalities. The deeply revolved and long-hoarded project of many years then declared itself in spite of diplomatic chicanery and plausible avowals of moderation. An able and well-informed writer (M. Schnitzler, " Secret History of Russia ") has said, that the future prospects of his country depend mainly upon the present emperor, and that it seems as if Providence had reserved great

things for him. The prediction may be fulfilled in
an inverted sense, as in the preceding example of
Napoleon. Instead of furnishing a parallel in
glory and success to the great Emathian conqueror, it seems more likely that he will pass into
a proverb with Nebuchadnezzar, Crœsus, Xerxes,
and Darius. The world cannot submit to be
periodically disturbed, but calls loudly for the
final abatement of an intolerable nuisance. When
the sword is once drawn it will not be safe to
sheathe it, until the common enemy is effectually
crippled, and we can apply to him in essence, if
not in reality, the words which Shakspeare puts
into the mouth of King Edward, when he brings
in his disabled enemy, Warwick, on the field of
Barnet :—

> " So, lie thou there ; and with thee die our fear;
> For Warwick was a bug, that fear'd us all."

It is well known, that the Russian autocrat rejected the recent pacific overture of the French
emperor peremptorily, and with sufficient want of
courtesy. He will not *allow* the Western powers
to interfere with what he calls his private misun-
derstanding with Turkey. As in a domestic
quarrel between man and wife, he considers the
interference of strangers unnecessary and imper-
tinent. When he hears of our preparations for an

immediate visit to the Baltic, he may say contemptuously, as his grandmother, Catherine the Second, did to the British ambassador in 1791, under similar circumstances: "As your Court seems determined to drive me from St. Petersburgh, I hope it will permit me to retire to Constantinople." *

Nicholas is either insane, blinded by systematic ambition, or urged on by fanaticism, and a belief that he is a chosen instrument to place the Greek faith above all other forms of worship, and to establish it as the true symbol of Christianity amongst the different races of men. All these causes have been assigned for his conduct, and either will suffice to carry out the probable consequences. The speeches which are put into the mouths of sovereigns in their desultory conversations on state affairs, are not much to be depended on, either as indicating their real sentiments, or as correctly delivered. If we can trust report, Nicholas has said, that Russia need not fear any coalition, and that after beating Charles the Twelfth, Frederick the Great, and Napoleon, her resources and armies are invincible. In this deduction, truth and falsehood are blended together in almost equal proportions. Some of the

* See " Progress and Present Position of Russia in the East." London, 1854.

abstract facts may be proved, but they bear neither resemblance nor parallel to the present state of affairs. Charles the Twelfth rushed incautiously to his own ruin, by holding his enemy in ill-judged contempt. The easy victory of Narva laid the foundation for the disaster of Pultowa. He fell more under his own mistakes than under the power or prowess of his enemy. Napoleon furnished a more memorable instance on a grander scale, and with less excuse, for he had the example of the Swedish monarch before his eyes, while at the same time he adopted, in many respects, and in leading points, the plan of campaign he so emphatically condemned in his predecessor. In either case, the natural obstacles, the elements, and the errors of the invaders, proved the most available defences of Russia. At Narva, on the 30th of November, 1700, ten thousand Swedes stormed the Russian intrenchments, and drove eighty thousand men before them like a flock of sheep. At Pultowa, on the 8th of July, 1709, an exhausted band of twenty-four thousand, containing not more than half the proportion of Swedes, attacked fifty thousand Russians, and almost snatched a victory, until fairly borne down and ovewhelmed by numbers. The king, unable to mount his horse from a previous wound, was not as usual at their head to lead them into the thickest of the fight; but issued his directions from a litter, to generals who acted without concert, and troops disheartened by the absence of a commander under whom they had never known defeat. At Borodino, with equal forces, about one hundred and twenty thousand on each side, the Russians were forced to abandon a fair field, selected by themselves to make their stand and cover their capital; and might have been utterly destroyed, had Napoleon listened to the urgent entreaties of Ney and Murat, and followed up the advantages gained, with his characteristic decision. For once, and in a most momentous crisis, he wavered and halted, when he ought to have rushed on with the overwhelming force of a thunderbolt or an avalanche. This unaccountable apathy has never been sufficiently explained; but the supposition of Count Ségur seems the most probable, that he was enfeebled by fever, and his mind for the moment prostrated by the sufferings of his body. It is certain that he never mounted his horse during this great battle, but despatched orders to the several marshals and corps, in conformity with the reports they furnished, as the varying conflict assumed different aspects.

It cannot be denied that Russia beat Frederick the Great, in the rigid acceptation of the term; since the annals of the Seven Years' War enumerate three great battles, in two of which they were successful. At Gros-Jagersdorff, or Nor-kitten, in Prussia, on the 30th August, 1757, Marshal Lehwald, with less than thirty thousand men, attacked eighty thousand Russians, under Field Marshal Apraxin. The combat was obstinate and bloody, both sides claiming the victory; but the advantage rested with the Russians, who occupied a well posted camp, fortified with a numerous artillery. Their loss was much heavier than that of their opponents; but comparative lists of killed and wounded are unsafe criteria by which to estimate the result of a battle. Marlborough and Eugene drove Villars from his intrenched position at Malplaquet; so did Dumourier dislodge the Austrians from the heights of Jemmappes; but in either case, the victors suffered much more severely than the vanquished.

At Zorndorff, on the 25th August, 1758, the King of Prussia attacked General Fermor, and totally defeated him with immense loss, although with far inferior numbers. The Russians fought with the steady resolution for which they are remarkable, and struggled hard to redeem the faulty dispositions of their leader; but they fell into irretrievable confusion, and left above twenty-five thousand killed, wounded, and prisoners on the field, with twenty-seven colours, and one hundred and three pieces of cannon. Their second line, as it advanced, fired upon the first, and did nearly as much execution as the opposing enemy. The soldiers plundered their own baggage, got drunk with brandy, mutinied against their officers, and made no distinction between friends and foes.

At Cunnersdorff, on the 12th of August, 1759, Frederick, relying on his former success, laid himself open to a ruinous reverse. With fifty thousand men, he ventured to assail Count Soltikoff, who commanded ninety thousand, and had the additional advantage of double lines strongly fortified. For the first six hours he carried all before him, and drove the Russians from their posts with prodigious slaughter; but making a desperate attempt with his exhausted troops on the last intrenched eminence, near the Jews' burying ground, his infantry were twice repulsed, losing many thousands of the best soldiers in the world; and his cavalry, hitherto irresistible, met with the same bad fortune. The king was so confident of final victory, that, in the heat of the action, he despatched couriers to Berlin, announcing a decisive triumph, and ordering a *Te Deum* in all the churches. The Russian empress, Elizabeth, after the result, directed a religious ceremony to be annually observed, to perpetuate the memory of this sanguinary combat.

The greatest generals have met reverses, and very few have been uniformly successful. He who has made no mistakes in war, has made very little war, as Turenne once observed, in reference to a vain-glorious boaster, who pronounced himself infallible. Wise heads have declared, that war is a tissue of errors, and the commander who commits the fewest, wins the greatest proportion of prizes. The result of battle depends on so many incidental casualties, that calculation is often baffled; as the dicer throws the very number which, in the table of chances, is the least likely to turn up. Frederick the Great, who, as a strategist, has never been surpassed in ancient or modern times, sustained three memorable defeats, and always through his own imprudence; this of Cunnersdorff, against the Russians; Kollin, on the 18th of June, 1757, where, with only thirty-two thousand men, he attacked sixty thousand Austrians; and Hochkirchen, on the 14th October, 1758,* where, with all his unrivalled talents and experience in the art of war, he suffered himself to be surprised and routed by Marshal Daun. Out of twelve pitched battles fought in

---

* On the same day were fought the battles of Jena and Auerstadt, in 1806.

his many campaigns, he gained nine. Napoleon delivered above forty, and lost but two great fields — Leipzig and Waterloo. Marlborough ventured only four, and won them all. His were pre-eminently the days of sieges; he conducted above twenty, and never invested a town that he did not take; sometimes, too, as in the memorable instance of Lisle, in the face of armies superior to his own. Wellington was foiled once in an important enterprize, the siege of Burgos, which political reasons compelled him to undertake against time, and with inadequate means. He was obliged to have recourse to sap, in the absence of an effective breaching train, — not from deliberate judgment or blameable imprudence, but from imperative necessity. As in the previous cases of Ciudad Rodrigo and Badajos, unless he could snatch the fortress away by a given hour, nothing remained to close a most brilliant campaign but a retreat to the frontiers of Portugal, and there to wait for a fresh lion's spring at a favourable conjuncture. The French general Dubréton, who commanded at Burgos, has not received the fair meed of fame to which he is justly entitled, when we consider the tenacity of his defence, and the consequences involved. The man who, with a handful of soldiers, could detain Wellington for thirty-four days before a fourth-rate fortress, and successfully repel five assaults, entirely changing, for a time, the overpowering current of events, was no ordinary chieftain, and his name deserves honourable mention from enemies as well as friends. Wellington commanded in eighteen general actions of the first class, and never left the field except as a conqueror. In a fair estimate of military pretension, the Russians had not more to boast of in their encounters with Frederick the Great, than in their late inglorious achievement at Sinope, which they have signalized by the prostitution of rewards and the blasphemy of a thanksgiving. In both cases they presented an overwhelming superiority of force, and destroyed mercilessly, with unflinching Asiatic barbarism. The stern necessities of war are bad enough when carried on in accordance with the laws of civilized nations, who spare and save foes that are incapable of resistance; but when signally violated from a mere thirst of slaughter, they demand a signal retribution. The massacre of Sinope will live for ever in future history as an act of unequalled atrocity, which supersedes the fate of Poland, commemorated by the poet of Hope, as the "bloodiest record in the book of time." When the Russian hordes threw themselves into the scale against the King of Prussia, he was battling for existence with Austria, Saxony, and France, all upon his hands together. They seized the tempting opportunity, and plundered without remorse the cities and provinces which for the moment could make no resistance, and laid his defenceless capital under contribution. There was little even in the shape of pretext, except that the lion appeared to be beaten to a standstill, and the hungry wolves were greedy for prey.

The present population of Russia, including all her conquests, and the countries under her *protection*, looks up towards sixty-five millions, and surpasses that of France and England combined. It increases more rapidly than is generally supposed; but being thinly scattered over an enormous expanse, is not to be estimated by a relative calculation of figures. In the United Kingdom there are two hundred and twenty-five souls to the square mile; in France, one hundred and seventy-five; in Russia, not more than three. At the same time, the geographical area of this unwieldy empire exceeds that of France and England, sixty-fold. Condensed population and ready means of transport, are the real ingredients of solid strength. This scale, and not the mere extent of territory, is the true measurement of power. When population increases in highly cultivated countries, such as France and England, it brings double nerve from a multiplication of resources within a limited boundary, produced by the augmenting ratio of industrial wealth. When it expands through the uninhabited wastes of Russia, where human life and energy are sprinkled almost imperceptibly over vast districts hitherto untenanted except by wild animals, or a few nomadic tribes who migrate periodically without fixed residence, the impression is too minute to be felt before the lapse of centuries. The new inhabitants derive from the land but little means of subsistence, and the progress of fertilization is slow and painful. On the other hand, the means of France and England are available on the instant. What with us is a question of hours, becomes with Russia an argument for weeks, months, and years. We do not mean to say Russia is either impotent or feeble, but she is not that overpowering colossus which she has been represented. It is true she has gone on from one success to another, and her grasp is insatiate. But she has been permitted, rather than is in herself irresistible. Apathy or incredulity has favoured her; but if the eyes of Europe are not now clearly opened, they will never again have so promising an opportunity. Russian gold is always actively at work, in addition to her cannon and bayonets. The Hungarian chief, Arthur Georgey, was apparently bought over, and betrayed the cause of his country. Had he not done so, it is by no means certain, that even with the aid of Russia, Austria would have entirely put down the Hungarian revolt. The flame even now, is but smothered, rather than burnt out. The author of the "Frontier Lands of the Christian and the Turk," an authority of good repute, has no doubt of the treachery of Georgey, and adds, as an eloquent commentary, that he was the only one of the Magyar leaders (who had not·sought voluntary exile) that remained unscathed, and is now living in a town in Austria, on a pension from the emperor. Russian gold in 1812 purchased the treachery of the Greek Murusi, who, while in the Turkish service, was secretly in the pay of Russia, and through whose diplomatic double-dealings, Bessarabia was filched from the sultan. It is some satisfaction to know, that, in this instance, the traitor was punished by the loss of his head. Russian gold bought Jussuf Pacha in 1829, when he basely surrendered the fortress of Varna, and uncovered the right flank of the Turkish army, posted in the defiles of the Balkan. Russian gold was profusely distributed by Prince Menzikoff in January, 1853, on his pretended errand to Constantinople; and doubtless is now working the calculated effect, in the revolt of the Greeks in Albania and other provinces.

The Turks, it is true, have been universally unsuccessful in their contests with Russia, since they circumvented Peter the Great on the banks of the Pruth, and let him off easily when he lay completely at their mercy. But they have committed greater mistakes since. In 1812, Russian diplomacy prevailed over that of Napoleon, and Turkey made peace with Russia exactly when she should have continued the war with double energy. The release of the army under Tchigagoff, threw a force upon the right flank and rear of the French emperor, which, had it been commanded by generals of tolerable capacity, would have rendered the retreat from Moscow impossible, and not a man could have escaped. If Turkey had then remained deaf to the cajolery of Russia, and cordially co-operated with France, she would not have been reduced to the state in which she afterwards found herself in 1829, when Diebitsch crossed the Balkan, and encamped on the plains of Adrianople. And thus a second time she allowed her foes to slide away when there was no retreat, and to advance, with their diminished powers, was certain destruction. At present she is not likely to repeat those fatal errors. She has a general of first-rate ability, a well organized army, and powerful allies.

There is little danger of a second Navarino, a second passage of the Balkan, or a repetition of the treachery of Bucharest and Varna.

Either of the two great Western nations, France or England, single-handed, is a match for Russia, with the rest of Europe neutral. United we can select our field of operations, and reduce her to listen to such terms as we shall think proper to dictate. Throughout her own extended territory, in the sandy plains of Russia Proper, in the steppes of Lithuania, in the deserts of Siberia, in the wilds of Tartary, she is inaccessible; we are not going to march our armies two thousand miles inland, without a defined base of operations, to perish in the snow; we have no intention of going to her, but we can confine her within bounds, and effectually prevent her from coming to us. At home, and in the wide circle of her own limits, she is formidable. In aggressive and distant wars, although insatiable in desire, she is weak in execution. She cannot produce in the field the large armies that are created in an ukase, and terrify the credulous by imaginary numbers. If so, how is it that they have never yet stood in battle array, or been concentrated on a given point in the hour of necessity? We read of eight hundred thousand men, and as there are no colonies to demand large garrisons, no distant

C

wars to operate as a perpetual drain, where are
they when their presence would overwhelm, crush
and annihilate opposition? At Borodino, in the
heart of their vast empire, retiring on their resources, and resolved at last to make a final stand
to save their capital, and fight for independence,
one hundred and twenty thousand was the fullest
extent of their muster-roll. Neither did they ever
exceed this aggregate in the successive invasions
of France, in 1814 and 1815. Moreover, the
Russian contingent would never have arrived at
all but for the subsidies of England. M. Schnitzler, whose work is generally correct and authentic in facts, as it is often sound in opinions, has
been misinformed, or is tinctured with prejudice,
when he says, " The assemblage in the *Plaine des
Vertus* (10th September, 1814) of a Russian army
of one hundred and sixty thousand men ready for
the field, struck with amazement the diplomatic
corps of Europe, who were present at the imposing
spectacle ; but such an exhibition of the military
strength of a vast empire alarmed them much less
than the invisible power and perfect moral influence which the greatness of soul and well-known
principles of the monarch who now reviewed his
troops had created." I cannot tell what were the
impressions of civilians and diplomatists to whom
I had no access, but happening to be an insignifi-

cant unit among many hundreds of military men of all nations who were looking on, I can testify, that as a mere military display we were neither petrified with amazement nor awe. No mistakes are so easily made as calculations on the numbers of troops estimated from a *coup d'œil*; the general belief was, that on this occasion they did not amount to ninety thousand, and the entire Russian contingent which marched up to Paris, subsequent to the battle of Waterloo and the second abdication of Napoleon, I was assured by an officer of the Russian staff, never exceeded, even on paper, one hundred and ten thousand. At this vaunted review, which had been long in preparation, and lasted three days, little or nothing was done to illustrate strategy or capability of rapid movement. Three days previous to the commencement of the display, were required to place them on the ground. On the first day of action, the operations consisted in marching past in review order; on the second, they were confined to performing worship according to the rites of the Greek Church; and on the third, the whole force marched off again to the cantonments from whence they had been summoned. Not long after this, in an after-dinner conversation, arising incidentally, the Duke of Wellington proposed to the Allied Sovereigns, or they suggested to him, to

shew them the British army with their allies in
British pay, including the Hanoverian and Danish
division, amounting in all to more than eighty
thousand men. A representation of the principal
manœuvres and incidents of Salamanca, as nearly
as the ground permitted, was afterwards stated to
have been the programme agreed on for the evolutions of the day. There was no previous announcement or rehearsal. At nine at night, the
orders were sent round to the different brigades,
and by eight on the following morning, the whole
were drawn up in two lines, the left resting on
Montmartre, and the right on the Seine, with
St. Denis a little in the rear. The Sovereigns
with a gallant escort, comprising many of the
leading generals of the day, rode hastily along the
front. All were then put in motion; the entire
day was occupied in a series of complicated movements, and at seven in the evening the corps
marched past the assembled potentates, and returned to their several quarters. The quickness
and precision of the evolutions, the martial bearing and exact discipline of the men, and especially
the equipments of the horse artillery, excited the
loudest approbation. It was a proud day for
Britain, as showing a solid exhibition of her
power. Thousands still live who will recollect
the impression it produced, and the reminiscences

will not incline them to join the ranks of despon-
dency. We have not at this moment, the same
numerical amount of men, for we have not
hitherto required them, but we possess a sub-
stantial nucleus of similar materials, which we
can increase at pleasure; now that a necessity for
the supply has arisen. The Russian Imperial
Guards, during the occupation of Paris, in 1815,
were chosen troops, well appointed and imposing
in appearance; but their ordinary infantry of the
line were anything but formidable. They had
neither muscle nor stamina. Sir William Napier,
speaking of this same army, says, " If we believe
those writers who have described the ramifications
of the one huge falsehood of pretension, which,
they say, pervades Russia, her barbarity, using
the word in its full signification, would appear
more terrible than her strength. Nor can I question their accuracy, having in 1815, when the
reputation of the Russian troops was highest,
detected the same falsehood of display without
real strength. For, from the imperial parades on
the Boulevards of Paris, where oiled, bandaged,
and clothed to look like men whom British
soldiers would be proud to charge on a field of
battle, the Muscovite was admired, I followed him
to his billet, where, stripped of his disguise, he
appeared short of stature, squalid and meagre,

his face rigid with misery, shocking sight and
feeling—a British soldier would have offered
him bread rather than a bayonet."* "The ave-
rage pay of the Russian soldier is about twelve
shillings per annum. In some corps, it is a little
more or less, but the difference only amounts to
a few pence per month. Instead of the substan-
tial broth and beef which constitute the daily
mess of the British regiment, his food consists of
coarse rye bread, fermented cabbage, and buck-
wheat grits, to which a little hempseed oil is
added. In the picked regiments of the Guards,
where the men are supposed to 'live like fighting
cocks,' they receive half a pound of meat either
twice or thrice a week. They are supplied with
quass, a drink no way intoxicating, as may be
inferred from the fact of a couple of slices of
sour bread allowed to ferment in half a bucket
of water, being the usual recipe to make it."†
With this liberal allowance of sustaining food, the
frame of the Russian soldier cannot be very muscular, and his empty interior is not much better
furnished than that of poor Tom in King Lear,
when, in the extremity of hunger, he howls out,
"*Hopdance* cries in my belly for two white her-
rings!" Our readers who have seen Russian

---

* Conquest of Scinde. Part. I. 1845.
† See Revelations of Russia.

soldiers under arms, or examined them individually, may satisfy themselves that the accounts given are not exaggerated. Yet they stand doggedly on the field of battle, and will face death with sullen resolution—the devotion of serfdom rather than the impulse of heroism. There is a spice of the Mohammedan predestinarianism, too, mixed up with their passive courage. They believe that a soldier who falls bravely in battle has earned his passport into heaven without absolution or intermediate purgatory. Their doctrine is submission, and they submit. Even in their barracks, they preserve a staid, subdued demeanour, which is the effect of iron discipline. They are never joyous and light hearted. When off duty, the song, the laugh, or the jest, seldom issues from their mouths, or brightens up their countenances. They have not the "alacrity of spirit," the "cheer of mind," which animates the British warrior, who has enlisted freely, likes his profession, is satisfied with his lot, and firmly believes, and intends to prove, when in the field, that he is a better man than his opponent, let that opponent be who he may. He considers fight synonymous with victory, and feels as confident of winning the battle he is about to engage in, as the sailor on the look-out at the mast-head of a frigate, who invariably shouts out "a prize! a prize!" if he discovers a three-decker approaching.

"It is true," says Mr. O'Brien,* a very recent observer, "that at times, in marching, whole battalions sing in chorus either the national anthem, which is a fine solemn air, or some wild melody generally of a warlike character, interspersed with sharp cries and an occasional shrill whistle. These latter songs are particularly animated and spirit-stirring; and the quick rattle of the drum, which is the sole instrumental accompaniment, increases their exciting character. To the listener, there is something sublime in thus hearing thousands of manly voices blended together in chorus, uttering sentiments of devotion to God and the emperor, or of fierce defiance to the enemies of the czar. But even in these exhibitions, the sternness of military rule is seen. Upon the faces of the men thus engaged, no trace of emotion is visible; their tread is measured; their forms are erect: they are obeying a command, and not an impulse. The emotions of the heart seem to have been drilled into order; and expressions of love or anger, devotion or revenge, are only awakened by the voice of their commander."

* Journal of a Residence in the Danubian Principalities in 1853.

The effect of martial music or melody is doubt-less of a very imposing character, and well cal-culated to excite the spirits of participators and listeners. We have heard the Russian national anthem, and others of their most popular airs, played by the bands, or chanted by regiments on the march, but we were not deeply impressed by either. They have nothing in them to compete with the majestic solemnity of our own " God save the Queen," or the brilliant anima-tion of the French " Marseillaise," " Vive Henri Quatre," or the " Veillons sur le Salut de l'Empire " of the old Imperial Guard.

The Normans advanced to the charge at Hastings singing the song of Rollo, their favourite chieftain, and founder of their greatness. On the plains of Lutzen, in 1632, forty thousand Swedish voices, led by their king, pealed forth " Luther's Hymn " in unison, and then rushed to the attack of the Austrian intrenchments. At Bannockburn, the Scots knelt in speechless prayer before the shock of battle. On observing this the English monarch exclaimed, " They submit, they sue for mercy!" " They do, indeed," observed one of his attendant barons, " but it is to the King of kings alone!" The stern silence of determination before the mortal combat, is more formidable in reality than the eager shout of anticipated triumph, or the loud clangor of military instruments. The one proceeds from patriotic devotion or constitutional courage, an innate resolve to do or die; the other is, in some respects, a fictitious excitement, which may subside as readily as it is provoked.

The Russian soldier obeys orders without reasoning on their propriety, or thinking of the consequences. He never presumes to question the wisdom of his superiors, and is no tactician like the lively, intelligent Gaul, who thinks himself as good a general as the feathered and decorated marshal who directs his movements. The Muscovite is constitutionally dull, and displays little excitement except when he anticipates a rich harvest of plunder. With honest Cuddie Headrigg, he shows that he is " not that dooms stupid when it comes to lifting."

Next to the commissariat, which is a nullity, the greatest defect in the organization of the Russian army is the inferiority of their regimental officers, many of whom can scarcely read or write, and command no respect from personal character. The private soldier is badly clothed, ill paid, worse fed, and totally neglected when in hospital, whether from wounds or sickness. On the opening of a campaign, no matter in what climate, or at what period of the year, the Russian hospitals, such as they are, soon become crowded with inmates, who seldom go out again upon their legs. In the meantime, the number of effective soldiers in the daily states remains undiminished, for all the authorities are equally interested in keeping them up to the full amount. The mortality from disease far exceeds that of any other European army. Their sick are as heavy an incumbrance as the camp followers of an Indian host. In the war of 1828-9, which brought Diebitsch to Adrianople, the Russians were computed to have sacrificed 150,000 men, not more than one-third of whom perished from death or casualties in the field. The rest were the trophies of the hospital. When a battle is reported to the Emperor Nicholas, his first question is, not "How many men are killed?" but "How many musquets are missing?" He estimates the value of the weapon far beyond that of the animated machine who carries it. The latter is furnished by the Boyars, the former he must pay for and replace out of his own pocket. An imperial ukase, without a checque on his banker, cannot create powder and shot as easily as it can supply the food for those philanthropic discoveries. The men are the least expensive components of the Russian army; hence they are furnished more readily than their equipments. A British soldier is a costly article. He stands the country in at least one hundred pounds sterling before he is competent to face an enemy. Half a Russian battalion may be sent into the field for the same money.

The government allowances in Russia are not insufficient in any of their military departments, but they never reach the purposes for which they are assigned. Every thing is done by contract, and thus from the ministers of state to the generals of divisions, the colonels of regiments, the inferior officers, and the subordinate provedores, all descends in a graduated scale of peculation, until the victimized soldier has nothing administered to him but infinitesimal doses of pay and provisions; and these he must live on, as complaint leads to no redress but the knout and Siberia.

An accute observer, Mr. Oliphant,* corroborates this statement in a very impressive passage, which we here subjoin: He says, speaking of Russian operations in the south, "In addition to the natural impediments presented by the configuration of the country, the absence of roads, and the rigour of the climate, all military operations are crippled by that same system of wholesale corruption so successfully carried on in the naval depart-

* Russian Shores of the Black Sea, in the Autumn of 1852.

ment. Indeed, it would be most unfair if one service monopolised all the profits arising from this source. The accounts I received of the war in the Caucasus from those who had been present, exceeded anything of the sort I could have conceived possible. The frightful mortality among the troops employed there amounts to nearly twenty thousand annually. Of these, far the greater part fall victims to disease and starvation, attributable to the rapacity of their commanding officers, who trade in the commissariat so extensively that they speedily acquire large fortunes. As they are subject to no control in their dealings with contractors in supplying their requirements, there is nothing to check the ardour of speculation; and the profits enjoyed by the colonel of a regiment are calculated at £3000 or £4000 a year, besides his pay. It is scarcely possible to apprehend at a glance the full effect of a process so paralysing to the thews and sinews of war; or at once to realise the fact, that the Russian army, numerically so far superior to that of any European power, and supplied from sources which appear inexhaustible, is really in a most inefficient condition, and scarcely worthy of that exaggerated estimate which the British public seem to have formed of its capabilities. It is not upon the plains of Krasnai Selo, or Vosnesensck, amid the dazzling glitter of a grand field-day in the emperor's presence, that any correct notions can be formed of the Russian army.

"The imperial plaything assumes a very different appearance in the remote Cossack guard-house, where I have scarcely been able to recognize the soldier in the tattered and miserably equipped being before me, or on a harassing march, or in the presence of an indomitable enemy.

"We have only to remember that the present position of Russia in the Caucasus has remained unaltered for the last twenty-two years, notwithstanding the vast resources which have been brought to bear upon this interminable war, to perceive that the brilliant appearance of the Russian soldier on parade affords no criterion of his efficiency in the field of battle; while no more convincing proof could be desired of the gross corruption and mismanagement which characterise the proceedings of this campaign, than the fact of an overwhelming force of two hundred thousand men (quere, on paper?) being held in check for so long a period by the small but gallant band who are fighting for their snow-clad mountains and their liberty."

This wholesale organized system of public plunder exceeds all that we have ever read or heard of, in the history of ancient or modern peculation.

Our own home practice is not without some shining examples, but they furnish the exceptions rather than the rule. Verres in Sicily, and John of Cappodocia at Constantinople, under Justinian, were honest administrators of finance compared with these insatiate bloodsuckers. Here is a true and satisfactory solution of the supineness of the Russian leaders in Wallachia, who cannot concentrate strength sufficient to drive the Turks from Kalafat, or attempt the permanent passage of the Danube. They poured into the undefended Principalities more than nine months ago; time was everything to them, that they might have the chance of crushing Turkey before her allies could come to the rescue; and yet they have been beaten in every encounter with the troops of Omar Pacha, and have looked for a long time on the Turkish lines without venturing a decisive assault. If they do not endeavour to strike a great blow before the French and English auxiliaries arrive, their inactivity is a confession of weakness more damaging than a total defeat. In fact, they have neither the forces they would wish the world to suppose, nor generals capable of handling them, if they were ready to march up to the Turkish intrenchments.

In a war with maritime nations, how can Russia avail herself of her only two commercial outlets, the Sound and the Bosphorus, within which she will be hermetically sealed by the overwhelming fleets of France and England? It is difficult to answer this question, unless it be true, as Sir Francis Head told us in 1851, on the authority of the Hon. Captain Plunket, R.N., that Russia could send *thirty* sail of the line to sea, before England could send *three*. Our readers will start, but they have no occasion to be under any apprehension. Matters are mended since that alarm trumpet blew such a foreboding blast, and the Liverpool merchants may rest assured that a Russian squadron will not lay the Mersey under contribution, seize the defenceless shipping, and pillage their well-stored warehouses. The Muscovite nobility are luxurious as well as rich, but their revenues are principally derived from kind, nor can they easily convert their hides and tallow into specie, if the ordinary channels of commercial egress are impeded by a fleet of screw steamers. There will soon ensue a paralysis of the body, unless a timely cure is applied to the head. Beyond all doubt the Emperor Nicholas is individually and solely responsible for the impending storm which will soon burst in thunder on his country; the feeling of all the world which is not his, is against him, and not even the autocrat of half that world, and the arbitrator of countless millions can stand up before the battery of public opinion, so heavily and so unanimously erected to oppose his wild pretensions. Sooner or later the crisis must have arrived, and most fortunate is it that he has brought it on when we are well prepared, and when an unexpected coalition between former rivals has linked them together in a bond of confiding amity. We may now fathom the secret of his obstinacy. He has excited revolt and revolution in Turkey, relying on his power to coerce Austria, and to neutralize Prussia; but he dreamed not of the possibility that France and England would join the flags in friendship, which for so many centuries had waved in opposition. Neither did the first Napoleon believe in this, when from his island prison he prophesied that Russia would never pause until she held the destinies of Europe in her grasp, and that there was no opposing power strong enough to prevent this consummation.

We have already quoted from M. Schnitzler; we must add a passage from his preface, emphatically important, and which should never be lost sight of, until the impending war has satisfactorily solved the problem. "The position which Russia is to hold in Europe, is the greatest question perhaps for the future to unravel; its solution will be of vital consequence to France, and still more so to Germany, on which country the empire of

the Czars will press with all its mighty power as
soon as Poland shall no longer oppose an obstacle.
(To Poland he might have added Turkey.) As
regards France, the question is one of preponde-
rance, of influence, of equilibrium; but for Germany, it is one of life or death, of independence,
even of nationality. It is high time to awake to
the perception of this menacing future which has
recently been so strikingly pointed out by Thiers
and De Lamartine; it is now incumbent on all to
study an empire, the position of which is calculated
to awaken such fears.

"The territory, once a desert, is now covered
with inhabitants, and in no part of the globe is
population more rapid. At the accession of Peter
the Great, only a century and a half ago, Russia
possessed but sixteen millions of souls; now she
has more than sixty millions! It is not chiefly
by conquest that she has gained this prodigious
increase; for during that interval the superficies
of the empire has only augmented to the extent
of a fourth. It is to the proportional overplus of
births over deaths that this immense addition of
population is to be mainly attributed; a fact
worthy of the serious consideration of all Europe.
The same multiplying ratio may be remarked in
the resources of the empire.

"At the death of the great reforming Czar, the

entire revenue scarcely exceeded two millions and
a half sterling; at the commencement of the
present century it had amounted to fourteen
millions, and at the present date it cannot be
computed at less than twenty millions. Nor need
we point to the gold mines of the Ural and the
Altai, to explain this mighty increase."

It may perhaps better be accounted for by the
constantly augmenting trade with England, and
the value of exports. All points connected with
the government of Russia are profound enigmas,
and the war, amongst other discoveries, will probably bring to a more reasonable level, the produce
of their boasted gold mines. If his treasury was
full, the Czar would hardly be compelled to have
recourse to an unpopular loan at the very outset
of a contest, for which he was so well prepared
with the vital sinews. It is ascertained, that he
has lately withdrawn all his money invested in
the French and English funds, and this, perhaps,
furnishes his chief capital for the coming struggle.
The Russian empire is of modern growth, although
of ancient origin; it was little known or felt in
Europe previous to the accession of Peter the
Great, in 1768. The sovereigns were first called
grand dukes, then czars, or kings, in the Sclavonian dialect; and in 1721, only four years preceding his death, Peter assumed the title of empe-

ror, or autocrat. Such civilization as his country possessed before his reign, emanated from a
very unpromising source—the Greeks of the Lower
Empire, a 'degenerate race, who had outlived
their courage, patriotism, nationality, and pro-
ficiency in the arts and sciences; with whom
religion had lost her regenerating power, yielding
to the control of despotism, and never daring to
assert an independent influence. Peter himself
had found it necessary to make the express declaration, in his commission of laws, that " Russia
is a European power." The battle of Pultowa
established and obtained currency for a fact,
which until that momentous event, was scarcely
admitted. Russia rose progressively on the decline of Sweden, who since that hour has subsided
from the lofty eminence on which she had been
placed by the victories of Gustavus Adolphus,
his generals and successors, down to the condition of a third-rate power, while the advanced
posts of her enemy look into her very capital,
from her ancient appanages of Finland, and the
islands of the Gulf of Bothnia. Finland was
wrested from Sweden by the late Emperor Alexander, in 1808, under the specious plea of protection, and to compel the King of Sweden to withdraw himself from the close connection with
England (so essential to the interests of his

country) and which power the Russian dictator
was pleased to denominate "the common *enemy*,
and disturber of the tranquillity of Europe."
Not many months before, he was receiving our
subsidies, and brought his armies up to Eylau
and Friedland with English money. At that
time he was fascinated by the genius of Napoleon,
and being bribed by the secret conditions of the
treaty of Tilsit, expected to divide the empire of
the world with France. His apologists have said
that he had no choice, and was compelled to
succumb to measures which he secretly disap-
proved; but the statement is unsupported by
evidence. The position of his affairs was far from
being desperate, and though defeated, he was not
shivered, as Austria and Prussia had been in 1805
and 1806. The plain fact appears to be, that he
coveted Finland to complete his northern frontier; he was determined to obtain the province
which was now offered to his grasp, and although
his commerce was certain to be annihilated for
a time, by a war with England, and the revenue
of his empire seriously diminished, he calculated
on retrieving that mischief at some future opportunity. Equally as unscrupulous as his predecessors and successor, he cared little for solemn
obligations, the faith of treaties, or personal character, where monarchical ambition intervened.

Chateaubriand has said of him (Congrès de Vienne, vol. i. p. 180), " Sincere as a man, in all that concerned humanity, Alexander was cunning as a demi-Greek in all that related to politics." Napoleon went beyond this at St. Helena, and pronounced him " a consummate Greek of the Lower Empire." Napoleon was no worshipper of truth, the very child of passion, and slave of prejudice; but in this instance, he has not departed from justice in summing up the character of his former friend. And what compensation did Sweden receive from the allied sovereigns in the sequel? Norway was wrested from Denmark, to punish her for unswerving honesty, and added to the Scandinavian kingdom, as a counterpoise for her most valuable, indigenous, and loyal province,—an act of legalized dismemberment, almost as iniquitous as the passive consent to the partition of Poland, and quite as fatal a mistake in the re-organization of the map of Europe.

The reigning family of Russia, the house of Romanoff, as it is usually called (Holstein-Gottorp would be the more correct designation), is of comparatively recent origin, and dates from Michael Feedorovitch, who was elected to the sovereignty on the extinction of the ancient line of Ruric, which occurred in 1598, after that race had governed for seven centuries. A troubled interval of fifteen years had been occupied by civil commotions, foreign intrigues, impostors and usurpers, who appeared and disappeared as rapidly as the characters in a melodrama. The Romanoffs were no more than distinguished nobles, distantly connected on the female side with the dynasty of Ruric; in the earlier documents and chronicles they are scarcely noticed. All that is known of their genealogy, has been summed up by Müller, a great Russian antiquarian, in the following passage (quoted by M. Schnitzler), placed at the head of his life of Field Marshal Chérémétieff, whose family, as well as those of Kolytcheff, Jakovleff, Konovnitsyn, and Neplonièff, had a common origin with the house of Romanoff.

" The genealogical books, which from very ancient times have been compiled, little by little, with the object of proving the high origin of the most illustrious Russian families, give the Romanoffs and the Chérémétieffs the same founder; whom they sometimes call a Verèque, sometimes a Prussian, and sometimes a German; names, all of which anciently designated one and the same people. They place his arrival in Russia, under the reign of the Grand-Prince John Danilovitch Kalita (the Purse), or of his son the Grand-Prince Simeon Joannovitch Gordiè (the Proud);

an unimportant difference, since the former
ascended the throne in 1328, and the latter died
in 1353. It is recorded that at that period, a
man of distinction, Andrew Joannovitch, sur-
named Kobyla, came to Moscow to serve under
the Grand Prince. On account of this surname,
his prosterity figure in the genealogical books,
under the name of Kobylin. As at that time the
crusading brothers were making war in Livonia,
in order to spread the christian religion, and to
advance their own fortune; and as Russia, at the
same time being pressed hard by the Tartars,
promised considerable rewards to men of proved
valour, it is permissible to represent the ancestor
of the Romanoffs and Chérémétieffs, as a knight,
who, a native of Germany, went first to Livonia,
and from thence to Russia to conquer the infidels."

From this knight of the fourteenth century,
lineally descended Michael Romanoff (Fœdorovitch), who was the son of a boyar, and owed the
crown to which he was called in 1613, to the
best of all titles, a free, unbought, and unpre-
judiced election. It was not personal ambition,
or the overwhelming influence of family con-
nections, that made him Czar; but the desire of a
nation—the same voice of millions, which has given
to Napoleon the Third the legitimacy he so ably
vindicates by a wise and patriotic government.

The genealogical tree of the house of Romanoff has little pretension to antiquity in the estimate of those desperate archæologists (and they are not few in number), who consider the Norman Conquest an event of yesterday, and in the enthusiasm of their researches, would get behind the Deluge, and with the advocate in Racine's comedy, travel back to a starting-point, " avant le commencement du monde."

The members of this dynasty succeeded to the throne in early youth. Michael was seventeen at the period of his election. He reigned thirty-two years, and died in 1645, aged forty-nine. His son and successor, Alexis, was at that time fifteen. His reign extended over thirty-one years, and at his death in 1676, he was only a few months more than forty-seven. His sons, Theodore the Third, John the Fifth, and Peter Alexiovitch (the Great), were each sovereigns at the respective ages of nineteen, sixteen, and ten. Theodore died in 1682, after a short rule of six years, and still under twenty-five. John, in feeble health and endowed with limited faculties, reigned nominally with his younger brother Peter; until his death in 1696, in his thirtieth year, left to that great monarch the sole care of consolidating, or we may almost say, of forming the most extended empire the world had ever

seen. He was then twenty-five, in the fullest
vigour of mind and body, with an iron constitution, an active enterprising mind, a thirst after
knowledge, and an indomitable perseverance.
Previous to his reign, Russia had been little
thought of in the councils of Europe, was hardly
recognized, and ridiculed rather than feared.
With him therefore begins the historical and
political importance of his country. Her earlier
annals may occupy or amuse the idly curious, but
will not repay the time and labour of investiga-
tion.

Peter the Great, as is well known, worked as
a labouring shipwright and in disguise, in the
dockyards of Holland, and at Deptford, in England. So deeply was he impressed with the
power of the English marine, that he was heard
to say, "If I were not Emperor of Russia, I
would desire above all things to be a British
admiral." He was the great benefactor and reformer of his nation, although unable to civilize
himself—a rare instance of profitable ambition,
all centred in the advancement of Russia, which
he steadily pursued and most successfully accomplished. In his public capacity, the title of
Great has seldom been more justly merited.
Peter governed alone after the death of John,
twenty-nine years, and died at fifty-three. His

reign and life, in duration, activity, and utility, may be paralleled with that of our own Alfred. But though living at a much later period, his mind lacked the high moral refinement, the clear sense of right and wrong, which marked the Saxon monarch. He deemed that happiness, strength, and prosperity, were concentrated in power; and that wealth was the only solid basis on which power could be erected. He cared for ends more than the means by which they were accomplished. Moral improvement he made secondary to national interest, and when the second was looked to, he began to think of the first. Alfred sought to consolidate and improve a small kingdom, by equal laws and an impartial administration of justice; Peter incessantly laboured to extend and enrich a large one, by encroachments on his neighbours, and by inspiring his people with the restless activity of commerce. The command of outlets, rivers and ports, was the constant object of his thoughts and enterprises. "The plan of his general policy was grand and comprehensive. To profit fully by the mighty streams of his country; to govern the Baltic, and turn it to account; to confine the Swedes to their peninsula; to enfeeble Poland by fomenting its divisions; to draw the largest possible profit from the decline of the Ottoman Empire; to bring under the sphere of his own predominance, the christians of Europe and Asia, who wore the yoke of the Turks or Persians; to spread his influence, and to extend his future commerce to those regions which with a lengthened line joined his own dominions, and even to go beyond them; to gain for himself weight and consideration in the affairs of the West—such were the projects of the great Alexis Romanoff, embarrassed and increased by all the difficulties which his passion for reform had heaped up around him."*

As much of this system, so deeply organised, as circumstances permitted, he carried steadily out during the time that was allotted to him; the rest he bequeathed to his successors, and subsequent history has shown how pertinaciously they have trod in his footsteps, and on what regular progression these great plans have advanced to fulfilment, though occasionally checked by the want of ability to understand, the absence of will to execute, or the temporary intervention of some counteracting agency.

Russia has been twice saved by invasions which threatened to destroy her. The real danger was more imminent the first than the second time. Had Charles the Twelfth advanced to the triumphant occupation of Moscow in 1709, Russia was

* See Schnitzler's Secret History of Russia, vol. i, p. 16.

gone, and the fortunes of Sweden would have remained high in the ascendant : a strong, united, antagonistic race, predominant in the north, might have limited the Sclavonian tribes to their deserts and steppes. The empire of Peter and the future fate of Russia hung suspended in the balance at Pultowa, which has been justly classed by Professor Creasy amongst the " Decisive Battles of the World." When Charles the Twelfth, who had never yet known defeat, advanced to his projected conquest at the head of a numerous army glittering with gold and silver, and enriched with the spoils of Poland and Saxony, Europe looked on, and, as Voltaire observes, fully expected that he would dethrone the Czar. To overtures of peace he replied haughtily, "I will treat at Moscow." "My brother Charles," said Peter, " affects to play the Alexander, but I trust he will not find in me a Darius." He had said before, after the sanguinary defeat of Narva, " The Swedes will teach us how to beat them at last." He waited his time patiently and the prediction was accomplished. On that fatal 8th of July, 1709, " the power and glory of the war" passed from Sweden to Russia, for ever, and Peter triumphantly exclaimed, that the foundations of St. Petersburgh at length stood firm. It is useless now to speculate as to how the map of Europe would have been arranged in 1854, had the result of this great trial of strength been reversed; but most assuredly we should have seen a different division of the north, and many states would have been spared the practical misfortune of having a neighbouring *protector* at hand, ready for any emergency, and eager to step in as arbitrator in ordinary, whenever a bone of contention foments domestic squabbles.

Peter succeeded to an empire which has been incessantly increasing in extent, wealth, population, and importance, and owes all these advantages almost exclusively to him. He appeared at the very moment when his character and rare abilities had the fullest scope for their development, and were particularly suited to the country over which he ruled. A more humanized individual could scarcely have adopted the measures necessary to humanize his people. He and they were made for each other, and what was personally unamiable in the man became a valuable ingredient in the monarch. Had he isolated himself on the throne, surrounded by the outward pomp of barbaric greatness, his people might still have fallen down and worshipped him with blind or pagan idolatry; he might have held them in the same abject servitude, but he could not have reformed their evil customs, have instructed them in agriculture, arts, navigation, war, and have exalted them from mere animals endowed with instinct, into reasoning men. He taught them discipline by the force of example, more convincingly than by precept. He worked as an artizan in the dock-yards of foreign states; served as a common sailor in his own fleets, as a private soldier in his own armies; raised himself by regular steps and degrees of promotion, up to the highest command, which he only assumed when qualified by practical experience. By a system so new, and at the same time so thoroughly intelligible, he induced his more than semi-barbarous nobility to learn and feel the value of subordination, administered in a lesson bitterly repugnant to their pride, and which they would have refused to receive from any other master or through any other method of instruction. He re-created his people, although he was unable to correct his own intemperate passions. Yet with all his moral obliquity, his habitual drunkenness, savage temper, and unbridled passions, he never committed such an act of deliberate atrocity as the revocation of the edict of Nantes, which signalised the reign of his refined and hypocritical contemporary, Louis the Fourteenth. The trial, condemnation, and secret execution of his only son Alexis (which rests confirmed by proof beyond dispute), is not to be justified; yet even in this dark transaction, he had more than the provocation of Constantine, and ten times beyond that of the gloomy bigot, Philip of Spain, under similar circumstances.

One of the boldest measures of reform adopted by Peter, but at the same time, one which for the moment increased his difficulties, was the abolition of the old regular troops of the empire, the Strelitzes. Like the Prætorian bands of ancient Rome, the Janizaries of Turkey, and the Mamelukes of Egypt, these formidable cohorts exercised an *imperium in imperio*, superior to that of the sovereign, and could at any time depose or murder the reigning monarch, although they never contemplated the introduction of a new dynasty. Peter set them aside with the strong hand, but the new levies with which he supplied their places were officered chiefly by foreigners, disciplined after an unaccustomed plan, and little to be relied on until repeated defeats had inured them to the trade of war. Finally they triumphed, attesting their martial qualities in a succession of hard-fought battles; often victorious, never surrendering a field without a stubborn contest, and now ranking high in the scale of European soldiers, about to measure themselves for the first time with the united chivalry of France and England. The result will show whether they have been overrated, or are entitled to their reputation.

Peter the Great was twice married. By his first wife, Eudocia Lapoukhin, the daughter of a Russian boyar, he had two children; the unfortunate Czarovitch Alexis, born in 1690, and mysteriously executed in 1718; and Alexander, born in 1691, who died in the following year. Alexis married in 1711, the Princess Charlotte Christina Sophia of Wolfenbüttel, by whom he left issue, a daughter, Natalie, who died in 1729, and a son, born in 1715, who under the title of Peter the Second, reigned from 1727 to 1730, the year of his death. The second wife of Peter was the celebrated Catherine the First, who succeeded him. By her he had many children, of whom several were born prior to their marriage. With the exception of a single son, Peter, who died before he had completed his fourth year, they were all females. One of them became afterwards, the Empress Elizabeth.

Catherine, the second wife of Peter the Great, whatever might be her other recommendations, had little claim to the virtue of chastity. Her origin was low, as she was the illegitimate daughter of a Livonian peasant. With no opportunity of education, she lived for some years in a menial capacity in the household of a clergyman, when she married a Swedish dragoon, who shortly afterwards went with his regiment on a distant expe-

E

tion, and never returned. She then resided with the Russian general Bauer, either as servant or paramour, a delicate question which remains involved in obscurity. Prince Menzikoff accidentally saw her, became enamoured of her charms, and received her from his brother soldier. While living with the prince, Peter noticed her, the obsequious vassal surrendered his prize, who thus became the mistress, and after some years, the empress of the great reforming Czar, over whom she retained her influence to the hour of his death, when she was proclaimed his successor, in utter violation of the solemn agreement by which the house of Romanoff had been placed on the throne.

Michael Fœdorovitch, who by the unbiassed choice of the principal members of the clergy, nobility, and commonalty, had been preferred to the princes of the house of Rurik, in 1613, received the crown on the express condition that it should descend hereditarily by right of primogeniture. Peter the Great, while yet writhing under the disobedience of his son, and in a moment when arbitrary passion subdued his cooler reason, by an ukase of the 16th February, 1722, disturbed the order of succession. He decreed that the reigning sovereign should retain the right of nominating his successor, without any

exclusive clause in favour of the Imperial family;
an act of folly by a wise man, almost amounting
to an aberration of reason. His infant grandson
was alive, and there existed no just reason why
the child should be deprived of his inheritance,
thus pursuing the father with vengeance beyond
the grave. From this fatal mistake originated
the long series of disorders, conspiracies, and
crimes, which signalised the Russian annals
during the eighteenth century, when revolution
was perpetually stirred up by plots within the
palace, and the crown became the prize of the
most subtle intrigue or the most audacious
violence. Catherine survived Peter, and enjoyed her single sovereignty only two years.
She died in 1727; aged forty-one. Her decease was hastened by an immoderate indulgence
in intoxicating liquors, the love of which she
probably acquired from her husband. The same
sympathy of taste existed between our own Queen
Anne, of glorious memory, and her spouse Prince
George of Denmark, but in no other respect did
they resemble their Russian contemporaries.
Whatever may have been the early irregularities
of Catherine's life, she devoted herself to her imperial husband, often soothed him in his wildest
fits of passion, and extricated him by her skilful

52 HOUSE OF HOLSTEIN-GOTTORP.

advice and influence, when he appeared irretrievably lost on the banks of the Pruth.

On the death of Catherine the First, the son of the Czarovitch Alexis, then only in his twelfth year, was elevated to the throne, under the title of Peter the Second. He reigned for three years, from 1727 to 1730, when he died suddenly, deposed and murdered. This youthful monarch was the last heir male of the younger branch of the house of Romanoff. To him succeeded Anna Joannovna, daughter of John the Fifth, the elder brother and coadjutor of Peter the Great, on the death of their father Alexis. She was born in 1693, and in 1710 married Duke Frederick William of Courland, but had no children. She reigned from 1730 to 1740. On her death, the crown passed for a short interval of a year to her infant nephew, Ivan Antonovitch, but was then wrested from him by his cousin, Elizabeth Petrovna, fourth daughter of Peter the Great and Catherine, who reigned in great prosperity from 1741 to 1761. With her the direct younger branch of the line of Romanoff became extinct, and the collateral house of Holstein-Gottorp assumed their place in the person of Peter the Third. This Ivan, we have here named, passed a miserable life of imprisonment, in various places,

and perished in 1764, during the reign of Catherine the Second, in the fortress of Schlusselburg,
on the occasion of the rebellion of Mirovitch, who
tried to deliver him. He was a Romanoff of the
elder branch by the maternal side; his father
belonged to the house of Brunswick.

The mother of Peter the Third was Anna
Petrovna, elder sister of the Empress Elizabeth;
his father was the Duke Charles Frederic of Holstein-Gottorp. He was thus the grandson of
Peter the First by the female line, first cousin of
Peter the Second, and with him commences the
collateral branch of the lineage of Peter the
Great. This unfortunate monarch was born at
Kiel, in Germany, and gave great disgust to his
subjects and the influential nobility of the old
school, by calling himself a German, and repudiat-
ing the title of Russian. In early youth, he was
married to Catherine, daughter of the Prince
of Anhalt-Zerbst, who had then scarcely completed her sixteenth year. They soon began to
hate each other with mortal antipathy; no two
dispositions were ever more thoroughly uncon-
genial. She possessed a bold, undaunted spirit,
with a masculine understanding. Peter was
coarse, grovelling, and mean, with no spark of
royalty in his composition. He gave himself up
to low society and to the most scandalous excesses

Catherine, even in her early youth, was by no
means remarkable for her virtue, but had not
yet reached that excess of impurity, which
obtained for her in her imperial licence, the name
of the modern Messalina. With the inconsistency
usual in such cases, each party reproached the
other. Catherine, stung by her husband's bruta-
lity, became still more openly indecorous in her
conduct, and Peter indulged in habitual drunkenness and debauchery to such an extent, that he
must have been deranged. He at length became
so infatuated by his disgust for Catherine and his
passion for one of his mistresses, the Countess
Woronzoff, that he had determined to divorce and
imprison the former, and raise the latter lawfully
to his throne and bed. Informed of his designs,
Catherine promptly took the initiative, and carried a grand *coup d'état*. She caused her husband to be seized, and sent as a prisoner to a
small palace about twenty miles from St. Petersburgh, where Prince Alexis Orloff speedily dis-
patched him, with the connivance, if not at the
positive command of the empress. This explosion
and catastrophe occurred in July, 1762, a little
more than one year after they had ascended the
throne; and in the course of the next month,
Catherine was solemnly crowned Empress of all
the Russias. Loud hosannas pealed to heaven in

pious gratitude from the mouths of millions, thanking providence for the blessing bestowed on them in such a sovereign-mother; and ambassadors from every potentate in Europe knelt in congratulation before the throne polluted by lust, intemperance, and murder. Yet she ruled well and wisely, following firmly in the footsteps of Peter the Great, with measureless schemes of ambition in one hand, and endless projects of improvement and civilization in the other. She patronized learning, encouraged education, affected philosophy, composed moral tales for the use of children, translated a code of original laws into German, wrote some dramatic pieces, discoursed with apparent unction on religious subjects, observed all the outward forms of piety, ordered a Te Deum when Suvaroff butchered thirty thousand Turks at Ismail, and converted each of her palaces into a monster seraglio. Immersed in pleasure, she never neglected business, and died with perfect composure and a tranquil conscience, surrounded by the great officers of state, the ministers of the church, and the familiar associates of her domestic orgies. Such was Catherine the Second, called by the Prince de Ligne, her biographer and eulogist, "Catherine the Great;" the grandmother of the late Emperor Alexander, and of the living autocrat Nicholas.

Many years after Catherine had reigned in undisturbed possession of the sovereign power, a representative of her late husband arose in the person of the celebrated impostor Pugatscheff, who bearing a strong personal resemblance to the deceased emperor, was in 1773, encouraged to pass himself for that monarch. He had served in the Austrian and Prussian armies, and possessed daring courage with very considerable abilities. At first his partisans were few, but they soon increased to a formidable number. He gave battle to the troops of the empress, defeated them several times, captured Kazan, the ancient capital of the empire, and gave ample employment to Catherine, her ministers and armies, for two years. At length, when apparently at the height of success, and threatening Moscow itself, he was betrayed by some of his own followers, made prisoner, tried, and executed, with many rebel leaders, in 1775. The adventures of this Russian Perkin Warbeck are little known, but highly interesting. They have lately been described from authentic sources, and form a most valuable portion of an agreeable work, written by Mr. G. T. Turnerelli, entitled, " Historical, Picturesque, and Descriptive Sketches of Kazan, the ancient capital of the Tartar Khans." In that work is contained an animated account of the rebellion of

Pugatscheff, together with much information respecting people, places, and events, as little familiar to the general reader, as the early annals of China, before the age of Confucius.

There are not wanting to this day, many in Russia, who contend that Pugatscheff was no impostor, but really the man he pretended to be. But the idea is an idle chimera, and is maintained by mere visionaries, in the face of the most conclusive evidence to the contrary.

Catherine reigned thirty-four years, and died in 1796, at the ripe age of sixty-seven. The list of her personal favourites is innumerable. They were generally chosen from their stature and muscular proportions, without much reference to mental capacity. Of these, Prince Potemkin exercised the longest sway, and enjoyed the greatest power. He was one of the most remarkable men that Russia produced, and exercised a mighty influence over the fortunes of his country. But he was personally unpopular, although his measures were successful. Perhaps the richest subject in Europe, with wealth exceeding that of many sovereigns, he died (by accident) in a ditch, into which he was lifted for ease, from his carriage, and placed under a tree by the road side, when seized with the pangs of death in the progress of a journey. Sejanus, Wolsey, and Buckignham, never revelled in the plenitude of imperial favouritism, to the extent, or for the time, that Potemkin did. Russia belonged more to him than to his Empress. His character was a jumble of inconsisteney, a mass of antithises, without solid foundation or a definite object. Count Ségur, who knew him intimately, has sketched this extraordinary individual with a graphic pencil.

"In the person of Prince Potemkin were collected the most opposite defects and advantages of every kind. He was avaricious and ostentatious, despotic and obliging, politic and confiding, licentious and superstitious, bold and timid, ambitious and indiscreet, lavish of his bounties to his relations, his mistresses, and his favourites, yet frequently paying neither his household nor his creditors. His consequence always depended on a woman, and he was always unfaithful to her. Nothing could equal the activity of his mind, nor the indolence of his body. No dangers could appal his courage, no difficulties force him to abandon his projects. But the success of an enterprise always brought on disgust. Every thing with him was desultory —business, pleasure, temper, courage. His presence was a restraint on every company. He was morose to all that stood in awe of him, and

caressed all such as accosted him with familiarity.
None had read less than he; few people were
better informed. One while he formed the project of becoming Duke of Courland; at another,
he thought of bestowing on himself the crown of
Poland. He frequently talked of making himself a bishop, or even a simple monk. He built
a superb palace, and wanted to sell it before it
was finished. In his youth he had pleased
Catherine by the ardour of his passion, by his
valour, and by his masculine beauty. Become
the rival of Orloff, he performed for his sovereign
whatever the most romantic passion could inspire.
He put out an eye to free it from a blemish that
diminished its beauty. Banished by his rival, he
ran to meet death in battle, and returned with
glory. He died in 1791, at the age of fifty-two."
The character is a duplicate of Dryden's Zimri—

"A man so various that he seem'd to be
Not one, but all mankind's epitome."

Invested with absolute power, for inscrutable
purposes, we may readily suppose that such an
ill regulated mind proved a widely extended instrument of mischief, and added a heavy burden
to the weight of human calamity. Potemkin lives
in history, but no respect attaches to his name.
He is notorious rather than celebrated, a
destroyer, not a benefactor. His immortality is

the unenviable fame of Erostratus, and has no particle of the pure renown of Aristides. He was buried at Cherson; but Paul, on his accession, ordered the body to be exhumed, and cast into the first hole that might be found. It was accordingly taken up and thrown into the ditch of the fortress, with as little ceremony as if it had been that of a dead dog.

During the reign of Catherine the Second was conceived, digested, and perpetrated, the most atrocious political enormity which sullies the pages of European history; we mean the dismemberment of Poland. As Talleyrand said afterwards, on another lamentable occasion, the mistake was, if possible, greater than the crime. France and England could have prevented this foul act; but blind to the rights of humanity and their own transparent interests, these two great nations closed their eyes in fatal supineness, while an ancient, gallant, independent nation was swept from the map of Europe, without an assigned cause, or even a plausible pretext. The idea was first suggested by the Machiavelian brain of Frederick the Great. The tigress of the North responded to it with a convulsive spring; and the gentle Maria Theresa, after a little hesitation, consented to share in the anticipated plunder. For a century before, the balance of power had been the great watchword in the mouths of the leading politicians of Europe, and the first article in their acknowledged creeds; but now the phrase and the principle were equally cast aside. Austria and Prussia had long been deadly enemies, and both hated Russia even beyond the detestation they cherished for each other. Yet they made common cause, conspired against a country they were each pledged to protect, and with shameless profligacy became leagued in a scheme of robbery on a scale of unprecedented grandeur, consummated by the sacrifice of half-a-million of lives. On the part of Austria, too, there was the additional sin of heavy ingratitude; for not more than eighty years had elapsed since John Sobieski and his valiant Poles responded to her cry of despair, and saved her capital from the beleaguering Turks, and the impending horrors of an assault. This act alone should have covered Poland with a protecting ægis, and least of all, had she a right to expect a deadly wound from the nation she had preserved. Russia, too, might have remembered that Sigismund the Second once gave away her crown in Moscow, anticipating a march which met with less success two centuries later; and Prussia, unless she falsified her annals, would find there that her dukes had long been subject to the Jagellon kings of

Poland, and bowed before them with submissive inferiority. But the circling wheel of time had placed weak nations in the posts formerly occupied by strong ones; and Poland had gone down, while Austria, Prussia, and Russia had risen on her decline. The growing evils engendered by an elective monarchy, a lawless nobility, and an enslaved population, were about to be illustrated by a memorable example. If any human being could be imagined less fettered by scruples of any kind, political, moral, or religious, where personal ambition was concerned, than Catherine of Russia, that respectable individual was the far-famed Prussian monarch, the great warrior, legislator, philosopher, essayist, historian, poet, musician, and free-thinker; compared to whom Richelieu was a timid novice in applying the doctrine that the end sanctified the means, and who was ready at any moment for a partition treaty with Satan himself, provided an increase of territory was to be obtained for his own kingdom. Maria Theresa was less eager, and some diplomatic ingenuity became necessary before she suffered herself to be warmly drawn in as a party to the nefarious project.

After the first division of 1772, when Poland was deprived of all her vigorous limbs, a miserable torso remained, with a nominal king, a shadow of independence, and the guarantee of *protection* from the spoliators. At the end of eighteen years, this remnant of what had once been a flourishing kingdom, began to think that internal reform might yet bring back decaying strength, and ventured the experiment of a new constitution. The object was exclusively domestic, and aimed at no change in the existing state of foreign relations. The Prussian monarch had treacherously encouraged the Poles, and promised help in case of Russian hostility. The latter power at once denounced the Polish reform as a declaration of war, and marched an overwhelming force into the devoted territory. Stanislaus, the king of Poland, was cowardly in mind and body; but Kosciusko became his country's champion, and although he could not save, he encircled her expiring brows with a chaplet of immortal glory. On the fatal field of Maciovice (Oct. 1794), he was wounded and taken prisoner; and Suvaroff, after butchering in cold blood 30,000 Poles, of all ages and conditions, subsequent to the capture of Warsaw, on the 8th Nov. in the same year, extinguished further opposition, and Poland finally disappeared from the list of nations. Frederick and Maria Theresa had long been dead, but the Empress Catherine still survived, and witnessed the full consummation of her long-cherished plans.

Twelve years passed over, and with them many stirring events and many changes in the arrangement of the states of Europe. On the 18th of Nov., 1806, a French army, flushed with the victory of Jena, and the utter annihilation of Prussia, entered in triumph the ancient capital of Poland, and displayed their standards and eagles on the ramparts of Warsaw. A general cry of exultation resounded through the land, the heart of Poland throbbed with anxious hope, and her resuscitation appeared almost certain. Napoleon hesitated, paused in the intention he had deliberately formed, and was induced to lay it aside altogether. Friedland enabled him to dictate his own terms; but the Treaty of Tilsit, signed on the 7th of July, 1807, contained no article announcing that a native Sobieski, a Poniatowski, or even the chivalrous French soldier Murat, was to number amongst the sovereigns of Europe as king of ancient Sarmatia. The great conqueror lost a great opportunity; to lose it again a second time, when the fortune of war a second time courted him to accept it. It was not that he was blind, ungenerous, or insensible to the devotion which the Poles exhibited towards his person, or the strong reliance they placed on his invincible strength. But he suffered other political considerations to sway him, and they all tended in a perverse direction. His paramount object for the moment was to cripple the commerce of England; he had lately issued his famous Berlin decrees, and he accorded easy terms to the Russian emperor, to induce him to co-operate warmly in carrying them out. He therefore contented himself with the erection of the grand duchy of Warsaw as an appanage of Saxony, instead of re-organizing the independent kingdom of Poland. Alexander, by a secret article, obtained leave to seize on Finland, although Constantinople was denied to him, at which he plainly indicated his dissatisfaction, observing that every man ought to possess the gates of his own house.

Five years rolled on in the unerring course of time, and the summer of 1812 saw four hundred thousand French warriors on the banks of the Niemen, preparing to throw themselves into the heart of Russia, and expecting to dictate the terms of peace at Moscow and St. Petersburg. Liberated Poland stretched out her hands behind them, and her hardy soldiers filled their ranks with comrades eager to partake their glory. That moment was the crisis of Napoleon's fate; and he

F

suffered it to escape. Had he paused on the
frontier, instead of madly rushing into interminable wastes, where he could establish neither a
sound base of operations, nor flanks to sustain it;
had he proclaimed the restoration of Poland in
its full integrity, promised Sweden to co-operate
in the restoration of Finland to her dominion,
and kept alive the Turkish war with money, men,
and military supplies, instead of suffering Russian
diplomacy to out-manœuvre and defeat him in
that all-important quarter (and it is difficult to
understand why he, who saw so clearly, should
suddenly become blind); had this been his course,
it appears almost certain that complete success
would have attended the enterprise, which ended
in his ruin. So long as Russia was crippled and
brought to her knees, it mattered little whether
the treaty of peace was signed at Moscow or
Warsaw; but, for the empty vanity of dating
from the Kremlin, he sacrified fifteen years of
unchequered victory, and surrendered sober judgment to the influence of fatality. Above every
thing else, it was madness beyond the cure of all
the hellebore in the three Anticyræ, to leave what
Talleyrand called the *Spanish ulcer* in active viru-
lence behind him. But argument was at an end,
when, in reply to the remonstrances of the Abbé
de Pradt, he led him to a window, and, pointing

to the heavens, exclaimed, "Do you see that star?" In the words of Lord Byron, "never had mortal man such opportunity, or abused it more." Since authentic history has recorded human transactions, the same power has never been placed within a single grasp. He had no necessity to hurry, time was before him; he was in the full vigour of manhood, not more than forty-three years of age; his empire was firmly consolidated, his allies faithful, for as yet they had no temptation to drop from him to the stronger side. If the first Napoleon had re-established Poland in 1812, instead of rushing into the jaws of an enemy he might easily have evaded—the climate of Russia more death-dealing than her warriors—and leading his matchless host to perish in the snow, the chances are, that he would have died in the Tuilleries, and not on the rock of St. Helena—the sanguinary struggle for Polish independence in 1830 would never have occurred, and the tyranny exercised by Nicholas over that devoted country would not be reckoned amongst the political misdeeds for which we may hope he is now called upon to atone.

Paul succeeded to the throne of Russia on the death of Catherine the Second. At that time, the empire had increased to eighteen millions of square miles, comprising thirty-three millions of inhabitants. The latter had more than doubled since the accession of Peter the Great, during the lapse of a century. Paul was born on the 1st of October, 1754, and consequently was forty-two at his accession. His parents had but one other child, a daughter named Anne, who died in early infancy. He was twice married. By his first wife, Nathalie, Princess of Hesse-Darmstadt (who died 1776), he had no family. By his second, Maria, Princess of Wurtemburg (who died in 1828), he had ten children, four sons and six daughters. They are as follow :—

Alexander, late emperor, born 1777; died 1825.

Constantine, born 1779; died 1831.

Alexandrina, born 1783; married to Joseph, Palatine of Hungary; died 1801.

Helena, born 1784; married to Frederick, Prince of Meklenburg-Strelitz; died 1816.

Maria, born 1786; married to Charles, Duke of Saxe-Weimar.

Catherine, born 1788; married first to Prince George of Holstein-Oldenburgh, secondly to William the First, King of Wurtemburg; died 1819.

Olga, born 1792; died in 1795.

Anne, born 1795; married William the Second, King of Holland.

Nicholas, the present emperor, born 1796.

Michael, born 1798.

Paul disliked and feared his mother. The reminiscences attached to her actions were too painful to allow of love or esteem. His temper was always wayward and violent, and soured by degrees into the intolerable extravagance and madness which led to his death. Long before he succeeded to the throne, he counteracted and opposed the policy of Catherine wherever he was allowed to do so. One of his earliest acts, when he became emperor, was dictated by sound judgment. He re-established the succession by hereditary descent in the male line, abrogating the decree of Peter the Great; and only on the extinction of every male heir, was the crown to devolve to a woman. In such case, the throne was to belong to that princess who, at the time of the decease of the last emperor, was his nearest relation; and, in default of direct heirs from her, the other princesses of the imperial house were to follow in the order of their relationship. Had Paul died immediately after issuing this decree, he would have done some good in his generation, his memory would have been tolerably respectable for a Russian emperor, and his subjects would have been spared the necessity of limiting his tyranny by strangulation.

Paul was eager for war. The doctrines of the French Revolution disgusted him; as a genuine autocrat, he held democratic principles in abhorrence; and had no sympathy for freedom of thought or action in any but himself. When the Emperor Francis appealed to his assistance, he very willingly despatched Suvaroff with twenty-five thousand men to sweep like a simoom across the north of Italy, while, at the same time, he lent eighteen thousand more to co-operate with the English in their projected expedition to Holland in 1799. He held the soldiers of Western Europe in little estimation; and thought with Cæsar, that his Russians had only to come, see, and conquer.

Suvaroff was nearly as mad as his imperial master; but he possessed a military genius peculiar to himself alone, and quite beyond the reach of ordinary criticism. He soared above all known rules, and succeeded, while common capacities sinned against them, and failed. His predominant fault was his utter carelessness of human life. So that he carried his object, he heeded not at what sacrifice; but he did carry it in the face of all opposition; and, with intuitive quickness, he seized opportunities as they arose in the heat of battle, and turned them to account with the rapidity of lightning. If he was not a great master in the science of war, he was a terrible instrument in practice, and struck with appalling energy. Parma, Trebbia, and Novi taught the French that they had no longer to deal with the heavy tactics of Austria, or with a general who regulated his movements by the measured scale of an Aulic Council. Moreau taunted Napoleon with being a conqueror at the rate of ten thousand men a-day: he might have applied the sarcasm to Suvaroff with superior justice.

The Russian chief affected inspiration to inflame the fanaticism of his soldiers, and thus bound them to him by the double tie of personal regard and religious devotion. When forced to fall back by the disaster of Korsakoff, who had been signally defeated by Massena at Zurich, Suvaroff flung himself in frantic passion on the ground, and implored his men to trample him to pieces, rather than give way before the enemy; but they took him up in their arms and continued the retreat. The veterans who served under Suvaroff used afterwards to boast, that their favourite leader was never *cold, afraid,* or *defeated.*

For his victories in the marvellous campaign of 1799, he was created a prince, with the honorary cognomen of *Italisky,* meaning the "over-runner of Italy;" as Diebitsch was afterwards denominated *Zabalkansky,* or "the Balkan passer;" and Paskievitch *Erivansky,* or "the taker of Erivan." The Russians appear to have adopted this mode of rewarding services in imitation of the ancient Romans, who gave surnames to their victorious generals from the countries they subdued.

In the sequel, Paul treated his hero with signal ingratitude, which preyed on his spirits, and caused him to die of vexation in 1800. We should think more highly of Suvaroff as a military chieftain, if we could expunge from his history the sanguinary leaf which records the butcheries of Ismail and Warsaw, on each of which occasions thirty thousand helpless beings were slaughtered in cold blood, when all resistance had ceased. His despatch, announcing the taking of Ismail, is the shortest on record, and was couched in a couplet, for he was a poet as well as a conqueror. The literal translation runs thus : " Glory to God and to the Empress ! Ismail's ours ;" — a volume of blasphemy and carnage compressed into nine short words. Another rhyming translation has been given as follows :—

> " Glory to God, and glory unto you !
> The fort is taken, and I am in it too !"

A rhyme seems to be no unusual formula in Russian official communications. When the well-known Admiral Puke (an Englishman) retired in

disgust, he thus announced his intention to the
Secretary of the Admiralty :—

> " I am sick of the service, so tell the Grand Duke,
> I've thrown up my commission—your servant,
>
> JOHN PUKE."

Suvaroff was created to be a Russian general.
His character may be traced more clearly, in the
extraordinary manual he composed for the instruction of his soldiers, than in a folio of studied
description. This document he termed . his
"Catechism." A literal translation is given by
Dr. Clarke, in the appendix to his Travels, from
which we have selected the following extract :—

"A Discourse under the Trigger." (The general
is supposed to be inspecting the line and address-
ing the troops.)

"Heels close!—knees straight!—a soldier must
stand like a dart!—I see the fourth—the fifth I
don't see! A soldier's step is twenty-eight
inches—in wheeling, half as much again. Keep
your distances well. Soldiers, join elbows in front.
First rank three steps from the second—in marching, two. Give the drum room! Keep your ball
three days, it may happen for a whole campaign,
when lead cannot be had. Fire seldom, but fire
sure. Push hard with the bayonet—the *ball*
will lose its way, the *bayonet* never. The *ball* is

a fool, the *bayonet* a hero! Stab once, and off
with the Turk from the bayonet. Even when
he's dead beware of him, you may get a scratch
from his sabre. If the sabre be near your neck,
dodge back one step, and push on again. Stab
the second, stab the third! A hero will stab half-
a-dozen. Be sure your ball's in your gun. If
three attack you, stab the first, fire on the second,
and bayonet the third—this seldom happens.
(Very seldom indeed, and is much easier said
than done.) When you fire, take aim at their
guts, and fire about twenty balls. Buy lead from
your *economy*. (The treasury of the mess. The
Russian soldiers buy their own lead.) It costs
little. We fire sure—we lose not one ball in
thirty; in the light and heavy artillery, not one
in ten. If you see the match upon a gun, run
up to it instantly; the ball will fly over your
head. The guns are yours, the people are yours!
down with 'em upon the spot, pursue 'em, stab
'em! Die for the honour of the Virgin Mary,
for your *mother*, (the Empress Catherine—your
father, if an emperor), for all the royal family.
The church prays for those that die; and those
who survive have honour and reward. Offend
not the peaceable inhabitant, he gives us meat
and drink—the soldier is not a robber. *Booty
is a holy thing!* If you take a camp, it is all

.yours. If you take a fortress, it is all yours. At
Ismail, besides other things, the soldiers shared
gold and silver by handfuls, and so in other
places; but wait for orders, before you fall to
booty !"

His instructions with regard to diet are
delicious. " Have a dread of the hospital. *German*
physic stinks from afar, and is good for nothing.
For the health, *drink, air,* and *food;* for the sick
food, air, and *drink.* For him who neglects his
men, if an officer, *arrest;* if a sub-officer, *lashes;*
and for the private who neglects himself, *more
lashes.* Brothers, the enemy trembles at you !
But there is another enemy greater than the
hospital—the d—n'd *I don't know.* From the half-
confessing, the guessing, lying, deceitful, the
palavering equivocation, squeamishness, and non-
sense of ' don't know,' many disasters originate."

Suvaroff had such an intense aversion to any
person's saying *" I don't know,"* in answer to his
questions, that he became almost frantic with
passion. His officers and soldiers were so well
aware of this singularity, that they would hazard
any reply instantly, accurate or not, rather than
venture to incur his displeasure by professing
ignorance.

This synopsis of instruction is a most original
compound of buffoonery, madness, and sound

sense, admirably adapted to the comprehension of the catechumens for whom it was drawn up. Suvaroff had as much tact as O'Connell, in suiting his harangues to the quality of his auditors. He winds up with good practical philosophy. "One wise man is worth three fools; and even three are little, give six; and even six are little, give ten! one clever fellow will beat them all, overthrow them, and take them prisoners!"

The ill-digested campaign of Holland in 1799, beheld English and Russian troops, for the first time, acting in concert. The fraternization mixed up badly, and both parties soon entertained mutual dislike, mistrust, and contempt. The Russians were clumsily commanded, and went headlong on like blind bull-dogs, without plan, concert, or support, until beaten back again, when they plundered and burnt all that fell in their way, people, animals, and habitations, on the right and left, in the front and rear. They resembled the Free Companions of the middle ages, in courage, license, and ferocity.

It was difficult to form any opinion of their generals, who appeared to concentrate all their notions of strategy in a rush and a "Hoorah!" Hermann was taken prisoner in the first engagement, and Essen, his successor, said little and did less. The combined force was under the nominal control of the Duke of York; but by the sapient ordination of the ministry, and as if to show that they had no confidence in their own selection, he was forbidden to venture on any movement of importance, without the previous sanction of a council of war; the most improved method of reducing a commander-in-chief to a cypher, and of augmenting the probabilities of failure.

To the British Cabinet, therefore, and their council of war, must be attributed the ill-fortune which attended all the operations after the successful landing at the Helder, and the capture of the Dutch fleet in the Texel. Our government had persuaded themselves, without any evidence much stronger than their own desires, that the inhabitants of the Seven Provinces were tired of French oppression, and panting for liberty. It appeared that they were more tired of the House of Orange, and judging by their conduct to our troops when they retreated through Holland to Westphalia, in 1795, it was an idle notion to suppose they would welcome the English as deliverers. On the contrary they received them at the point of the bayonet, and made common cause with the French, on whom they placed the greater reliance. Many of our previous continental expeditions had shown that we were migratory birds of passage, who came and went according to perpetually shifting circumstances. In this abortive attempt to win back Holland, the force employed, although of discordant materials, was adequate to the purpose, and the opposing generals, Brune and Vandamme, were not men of first-rate pretensions. There was nothing in their names or reputation equal to solid legions on the day of battle. Yet a campaign in which thirty-eight thousand troops took the field against twenty-five thousand, terminated in three months, by the former entering into a capitulation to evacuate, by a given day, the country they ought to have conquered; and the military character of England, as far as regarded her capability of conducting war on the grand scale, received a shock, which a long succession of triumphs, from Alexandria to Waterloo, with difficulty retrieved. This is a distasteful reminiscence, but there is little wisdom in an attempt to disguise or "burke" the truth. The lessons taught by defeat, if properly applied, are often more valuable than those derived from victory.

The Russian emperor, vexed and disappointed at the result of affairs in Italy and Holland, in the wayward restlessness of insanity, imagined, as madmen usually do, that he was betrayed by his friends. Accordingly, he veered round, beginning now to admire the French in proportion as he had

formerly detested them. Perhaps his actual aberration of mind was greatly increased by these
unexpected disasters. Be that as it may, England
now became the perpetual nightmare which disturbed his dreams, and the object of his waking
antipathy. The French government was not slow
to profit by this sudden change in the sentiments
of the unsteady autocrat, and strenuously promoted the Northern Confederacy, which Paul
openly joined, and placed himself at the head of,
in November 1800, having previously laid an em-
bargo on British property in Russia. His mind
seemed for the moment to be concentrated on
devising petty schemes of annoyance against the
English residents at the capital. From these,
even the ambassador, Sir Charles (afterwards Lord)
Whitworth, was not exempt. The sledge of Count
Razumousky, who had offended him, was, by the
Emperor's order, broken into small pieces, while
he stood by and directed the work. It happened
to be of a blue colour, and the count's servants
wore red liveries. Upon which an ukase was immediately published, prohibiting throughout the
empire of all the Russias, the use of blue in orna-
menting sledges, and of red liveries. In consequence of this sage decree, the British Ambassador and many others were compelled to change
their equipages. One evening, at his theatre in

the palace of the Hermitage, a French piece was performed, in which the story of the English gunpowder plot was introduced. The Emperor was observed to listen to it with earnest attention, and as soon as it was over he ordered all the vaults beneath the palace to be searched.

His wild eccentricities would have been sometimes amusing, but that they were never divested of cruelty or mischief. Coming down the street called the Perspective, he perceived a nobleman who was taking his walk, and had stopped to look at some workmen who were planting trees by the monarch's order. "What are you doing?" said the Emperor, "Merely seeing the men work," replied the nobleman; "Oh, is that your employment? Take off his pelisse and give him a spade! There, now work yourself!"

The present Emperor Nicholas, some time since, driving along in his droshky, observed an English gentleman move down another street, apparently, as he thought, to avoid him. He sent an officer to ask why he had done so when the emperor was coming. The answer was, "that he did not see his Imperial Majesty." "Then desire him to wear spectacles in future," was the immediate command, with which the delinquent was forced to comply during the remainder of his residence in St. Petersburgh, much to his own annoyance and the amusement of his friends, for he was a remarkably well-looking man, and piqued himself on his clear sight.

Paul was perhaps the ugliest specimen of humanity that had ever been seen, which was the more singular, as his children, with the exception of the Grand Duke Constantine, were all eminently handsome. His wife, the Princess of Wirtemburg, was a woman of great beauty, highly endowed in qualities of mind. The present Emperor has always been accounted the finest looking man in Europe, and Alexander excited much admiration from his prepossessing exterior when he visited England, in 1814. Their sister also, the Duchess of Oldenburgh, was approved of even by the fastidious taste of George the Fourth. The Calmucks are a hideous race, but the physiognomy of Paul far exceeded ordinary Calmuck ferocity and brutish expression. When enraged, he lost all command of himself, which occasionally gave rise to ludicrous scenes. The courtiers knew very well when the storm was gathering, by a trick the Emperor had in those moments, of blowing from his under-lip against the end of his short nose. In the rare intervals of better temper his good humour was betrayed by an uncouth way of swinging his legs and feet about in walking. Upon these occasions his conversation was silly, and too grossly indecent to be listened to by ears polite. If women were present his language became more offensive than ever. Everybody throughout the empire was under surveillance, and "suspected of being suspicious." A request to leave the country entailed banishment to Siberia or to the mines. If any family received visitors of an evening; if four people were seen walking together; if any one spoke too loud, or whistled, or sang, or looked inquisitive, or examined any public building with attention, or appeared thoughtful, or stopped to gaze round him, or stood still in the streets, or walked too fast or too slow, he was liable to be cross questioned as to his motives, to be reprimanded and insulted by the authorities. The dress of Englishmen in particular was regulated by the police. They were ordered to wear a three-cornered hat, or, as a substitute, a round hat pinned up with three corners; a long queue measured to the eighth of an inch, with a curl at the end ; a single-breasted coat and waistcoat; buckles at the knees, and in the shoes instead of strings. Orders were given to arrest any person who should be found wearing pantaloons. An English servant was dragged from behind a sledge and caned in the streets, for having too thick a neckcloth, and if it had been too thin, that pretext would have been used for a similar punishment. After every precaution, the dress when put on, never satisfied the police or the Emperor—either the hat was not put on straight, or the hair was too short, or the coat was not cut square enough. A lady at court wore her hair rather lower on the neck than was consistent with the ukase, whereupon she was ordered into close confinement to be fed on bread and water. A gentleman's hair fell a little over his forehead while dancing at a ball, upon which a policeman with loud abuse told him, that if he did not instantly cut his hair he would find a soldier who should shave his head.

When the ukase first appeared concerning the form of the hat, the son of an English merchant, with a view to baffle the police, appeared in the streets of St. Petersburgh, having on his head an English hunting cap, at sight of which the authorities were puzzled. What could this mysterious integument be? "It was not a cocked hat," they said, "neither was it a round hat." In their embarrassment they reported the affair to the Emperor, who was as much confounded as his officials. A new ukase became indispensable. Accordingly a fresh ordinance was promulgated and levelled at the hunting cap; but not knowing how to describe the anomaly, the decree announced, that no person on pain of death should appear in public with *the thing on his head* worn by the merchant's son. An order against wearing boots with coloured tops was most rigorously enforced. The police officers stopped a foreigner driving through the streets in a pair of English top boots. This gentleman expostulated with them, saying that he had no others, and certainly would not cut off the tops of his boots. Upon which, the officers, each seizing a leg as he sat in his droshky, fell to work and drew off his boots, leaving him to go barefooted home.* All letters were opened, and if they contained any unintelligible or difficult passage, it was immediately construed into direct treason, and the writer hurried to Siberia without examination. It was impossible that this state of affairs could last long. On the 2nd of April, 1801, Lord Nelson shook the Northern Confederacy to its basis, by the bombardment of Copenhagen and the capture of the Danish fleet; but before he could arrive to repeat the lesson at Cronstadt, the Russians had taken matters into their own hands and strangled their Emperor. No one was surprised, for the event had long been anticipated. If it was ever lawful to bring about good by unholy means, this instance furnishes the exception. The restoration of peace with England followed as a matter of course.

The death of the Emperor Paul stands boldly

* See Clarke's Travels.

out as a prominent and characteristic episode in the history of Russia. The event furnishes a salutary warning to his successors, and a subject of profitable study for autocrats in general. The circumstances are not commonly remembered at present, it may therefore be considered neither uninteresting nor superfluous to introduce a short summary of them, derived from sources which have been relied on as authentic.

It is only necessary to glance at the intrigues of the French politicians, Messrs. Otto, Sieyes, and Talleyrand, who at that time formed a diplomatic trio, or rather were spies, at the court of St. Petersburgh. Under their directions, a captivating French actress, Madame Chevalier, was employed to estrange the Emperor from his family, and to create a temporary and terrible change in the affairs of Europe. He saw and became enamoured of the syren, who speedily established herself as the sole idol of his shattered mind, which she moved according to the direction of her secret principals, until Paul withdrew from his alliance with Austria, recalled Suvaroff and his all-conquering army, crowded the roads to Siberia with British subjects, and filled with terror and consternation the exchange of the British empire.

The conspirators were few in number, but reso-

lute in purpose; they were men of rank and
influence, actuated by no other motive than to
prevent the final ruin of their country, and for
this purpose they hesitated not to place in peril
their lives and fortunes. In their conferences,
which were managed with admirable discretion,
it was resolved that Paul should die: and like
Cæsar, it was also destined that he should perish
in the ides of March, on the day of the festival
called Maslaintza. The Emperor, from the aversion which he had taken to those palaces which
formed the favourite residences of his mother,
resolved upon building a new one for himself.
The gorgeous magnificence of the Zarsko Zelo,
and of the Winter Palace, and all the oriental
voluptuousness of the Hermitage, were hateful
to him. Indeed, to such a height had his abhorrence of these places attained, that he had determined to reduce them to the dust, that only

"The blackness of ashes should mark were they stood."

His fate, which was fast approaching, prevented
the accomplishment of this irretrievable act of
delirium. The Emperor and his family resided,
at the time when the confederacy had resolved
upon his removal, in the new palace of St. Michael.
This is an enormous quadrangular pile, of red
Dutch brick, rising from a massive basement of

hewn granite; it stands at the bottom of the summer gardens, and the lofty spire of its Greek chapel, richly gilded with ducat gold, rising above the trees, has a beautiful appearance.

As Paul was anxious to inhabit this palace as soon after he was crowned as possible, the masons, the carpenters, and various artificers, toiled with incredible labour by day and by torch-light under the sultry sun of the summer, and in all the severity of a polar winter, so that in three years this enormous and magnificent fabric was completed. The whole is moated round, and when the stranger surveys its bastions of granite and numerous drawbridges, he is naturally led to conclude that it was intended as the last asylum of a prince at war with his subjects. Those who have seen its solid walls, and the capaciousness and variety of its chambers, will easily admit that an act of violence might be committed in one room, and not be heard by those who occupy the adjoining one; and that a massacre might be perpetrated at one end and not known at the other.

Paul took possession of this palace as a place of strength, and beheld it with rapture, because his imperial mother had never seen it.

Whilst his family were here, by every act of tenderness, endeavouring to soothe the terrible perturbation of his mind, there were not wanting those who exerted many stratagems to inflame and increase it. These people were constantly insinuating that every hand was armed against him. With this impression, which added fuel to his burning brain, he ordered a secret staircase to be constructed, which, leading from his own chamber, passed under a false stove in the ante-room, and led by a small door to the terrace.

It was the custom of the Emperor to sleep in an outer apartment, next to the Empress's, upon a sofa, in his regimentals and boots, whilst the Grand Duke and Duchess, and the rest of the Imperial family, were lodged at various distances, in apartments below the story which he occupied. On the 23rd day of March, N.S., 1801, the day preceding the fatal night, (whether Paul's apprehension, or anonymous information, suggested the idea, is not known, but conceiving that a storm was ready to burst upon him) he sent to Count P——, the governor of the city, one of the noblemen who had resolved on his destruction: "I am informed, P——," said the Emperor, "that there is a conspiracy on foot against me, do you think it necessary to take any precaution?" The Count, without betraying the least emotion, replied, "Sire, do not suffer such apprehensions to haunt your mind; if there were any combinations forming against your Majesty's person, I am sure I should be acquainted with them." "Then I am satisfied," said the Emperor; and the governor withdrew.

Before Paul retired to rest, he unexpectedly expressed the most tender solicitude for the Empress and his children, kissed them with all the warmth of farewell fondness, and remained with them longer than usual; and after he had visited the sentinels at their different posts, he retired to his chamber, where he had not long remained, before, under some colourable pretext that satisfied the men, the guard was changed by officers who had the command for the night, and were engaged in the confederacy. An hussar, whom the Emperor had particularly honoured by his notice and attention, always at night slept at his bed-room door, in the ante-room. It was impossible to remove this faithful soldier by any fair means.

At this momentous period silence reigned throughout the palace, except where it was disturbed by the pacing of the sentinels, and only a few lights were to be seen distantly and irregularly gleaming through the windows of this dark, colossal abode. In the dead of the night Z—— and his friends, amounting to eight or nine persons, passed the drawbridge, easily ascended the staircase which led to Paul's chamber, and met with no resistance till they reached the ante-room, when the faithful hussar, awakened by the noise, challenged them, and presented his piece. Much as they must all have admired the brave fidelity of the guard, neither time nor circum-stances would admit of an act of generosity, which might have endangered the whole plan. Z—— drew his sabre, and cut the poor fellow down. Paul, awakened by the noise, sprang from his sofa. At this moment the whole party rushed into the room. The unhappy sovereign, anticipating their design, at first endeavoured to intrench himself with the chairs and tables; then recovering, he assumed a high tone, told them they were his prisoners, and called upon them to surrender. Finding that they fixed their eyes steadily and firmly upon him, and continued advancing towards him, he implored them to spare his life; declared his consent instantly to relinquish the sceptre, and to accept of any terms which they would dictate. In his raving he offered to make them princes, and to give them estates, and titles, and orders without end. They now began to press more closely upon him, when he made a convulsive effort to reach the window. In the attempt he failed, and indeed, so high was it from the ground that had he succeeded, the expedient would only have put a more instantaneous period to his misery. In the effort he severely cut his hand with the glass, and as they drew him back he grasped a chair, with which he felled one of the assailants, and a desperate resistance took place. So great was the noise, that notwithstanding the massy walls and thick double folding-doors which divided the apartments, the Empress was disturbed, and began to cry for help, when a voice whispered in her ear, and imperatively told her to remain quiet, otherwise, if she uttered another word, she should be put to instant death. Whilst the Emperor was thus making a last struggle, the prince Y—— struck him on one of his temples with his fist, and laid him upon the floor. Paul, recovering from the blow, again implored his life. At this moment the heart of P—— Z—— relented, and upon being observed to tremble and hesitate, a young Hanoverian resolutely exclaimed, "We have passed the Rubicon, if we spare his life, before the setting of to-morrow's sun we shall be victims!" Upon which he took off his sash, turned it twice round the naked neck of the Emperor, and giving one end to Z——, and holding the other himself, they pulled for a considerable time with all their force, until their miserable sovereign was no more. They then

retired from the palace without the least moles-
tation, and returned to their respective homes.

What occurred after their departure can be
better conceived than depicted. Medical aid was
resorted to, but in vain; and upon the breathless
body of the Emperor fell the tears of his widowed
Empress, and children, and domestics. The sun
shone upon a new order of things. At seven
o'clock the intelligence of the decease of Paul
spread through the capital. The interval of time
from its first communication to its diffusion over
every part of Petersburgh, was scarcely percept-
ible. Joy and confidence, which had long been
strangers, mantled upon every face. At the
parade Alexander presented himself on horseback,
when the troops hailed him with loud and cordial
acclamations.

What followed is of a very subordinate consideration; but perhaps it will be eagerly asked to
what extremity did the avenging arm of Justice
pursue the perpetration of the deed? A conviction that the reigning motive was the salvation of
the empire, restrained her from being vindictive.
P—— Z—— was ordered not to approach the
imperial residence, and the governor of St. Petersburgh was transferred to Riga. When did regicides
ever escape so easily? As soon as Madame Chevalier was informed of the death of her imperial

patron, she prepared, under the protection of her brother, a dancer, for flight, with a booty of nearly a million of roubles. A police officer was sent to inspect and report upon her property. Amongst a pile of valuable articles, he discovered a diamond cross of no great intrinsic value, which had been given by Peter the First to a branch of the imperial family, and on that account much esteemed. It was to recover this that the officer was sent, who obtained it, after the most indecent and unprincipled resistance on her part. Passports were then granted to Madame Chevalier and her brother, and thus terminated this extraordinary and impressive tragedy.

The details of the murder of the emperor Paul bore some resemblance to those which attended the similar catastrophe of the Marquis Monaldeschi, who was assassinated in the palace of Fontainebleau by order of Queen Christina of Sweden. But the one was an act of private vengeance arising from woman's jealousy; the other a deed of public retribution excited by the sufferings of an enraged nation.

On the death of Paul, his eldest son Alexander succeeded to the throne amidst the universal rejoicings and congratulations of his subjects. Even with the conspirators there was no question of changing the dynasty: their only object was to get rid of the tyrant. Born on the 22nd December, 1777, Alexander had only completed his twenty-fourth year. Although personally brave, he was constitutionally a lover of peace, and had a natural dislike to war and bloodshed. Educated by Casar Laharpe, a republican, and a sort of latitudinarian philosopher, he had acquired respectable humanity without imbibing much regard for religion.

The burning of Moscow, and the result of the campaign of 1812, began to impress his mind with sincere piety, which was afterwards strengthened and confirmed by many conversations with the strange visionary Madame Krudener. At one time a brilliant leader of fashion in Paris, this singular woman merged into a fanatical devotee, and wandered about the world preaching and prophesying. After announcing the millennium to the Swiss mountaineers, she was hunted by the police from one State to another, and finally died in the Crimea, in 1824. The emperor declined inviting her to Moscow or St. Petersburgh to revive their sublimated lucubrations.

Alexander had many requisites to command and retain popularity; his manners were polished, his mind cultivated, and his personal appearance imposing. Everything seemed to predict to him a

long life-rent of the temporal glory he reached
when young, and from which he was suddenly
removed at the early age of forty-eight.

Many attempts have been made to implicate
him in the murder of his father, as it has often
been said that he was assassinated himself. The
two inferences are equally without foundation.
Napoleon, at St. Helena, accused him of direct
participation in the death of Paul, and produced
in evidence the fact that he placed on his personal
staff, one of the most active conspirators, and
treated him with unusual confidence. The truth
appears to be, that Alexander was cognizant of
what was intended, but utterly unable to prevent
it. Interference on his part, without saving his
father, would have entailed his own destruction
and the ruin of the family. His feelings as a son
and a man, revolted from the manner of the deed,
although reason must have forced him to admit
that it was politically inevitable. Whether he can
be justly charged with moral obliquity, or indirect
connivance, is an open question which has been
freely discussed.

When Charles the First was brought to trial,
his son, then Prince of Wales, remitted to the
parliament a blank paper with his signature
attached, and bound himself under a solemn pro-
mise to abide by any conditions they might please

to insert as regarded himself, provided only the life of his father was spared. Here was a flourish of magnanimity which reads well as an anecdote. Alexander certainly did not follow the example, but submitted to circumstances without useless remonstrance. In this critical moment of his life, he evinced little disposition to a personal sacrifice, but the cases are scarcely parallel, and in a general estimate of either public or private character, it would be a libel on the memory of the Russian monarch to reduce him to a level with the restored Stuart. Paul was disposed of, and Russia, with all Europe, were gainers by the exchange—

> " No matter *how*—he slept among the dead,
> And Alexander reigned in his stead." *

Alexander was married at sixteen to the Princess Louise-Marie-Auguste of Bavaria, who had not completed her fifteenth year. At the nuptials, which took place on the 9th of October, 1793, she was required to change the form of her religion, from the Romish to the Greek church; and on the ceremony of renunciation, received, with the holy ointment, the name of Elizabeth Alexeiovna, by which she was afterwards known and universally revered. They had two daughters who died young and left them childless. Alexander, who was of inconstant temperament, deserted his lovely

---

* Churchill.

and accomplished wife, for the variety of a succession of mistresses, by one of whom he had three children, who also preceded him to the grave.

His intrigues, although sufficient to render the empress unhappy, occasioned little public scandal, as they were not unblushingly paraded, but carried on in profound secrecy. Hence he obtained a reputation for moral propriety and domestic virtue without much claim, and in the reality of which his brother Nicholas is infinitely his superior. At the commencement of his reign, he dedicated his thoughts to peace and the internal improvement of his vast empire. In 1803, he offered his mediation between France and England, but without effect. Turkey obtained a respite, but not a release. The designs of Russia in the east were suspended rather than abandoned, and the ominous finger-post, erected by Catherine the Second at Cherson, still remained with the inscription "The way to Constantinople." His coronation at Moscow was signalised by acts of amnesty, which contrasted well with the tyranny of Paul. He diminished taxes, liberated debtors, prohibited prosecutions for the recovery of fines, and granted a free pardon to all deserters from the army. But one giant grievance he left untouched, and lacked the firmness to grapple with—public corruption. In every office of the state, from the prime minister

H

down to the lackeys of the clerks, he checked cruelty, but he shrank from reform. On this point a well informed author,* who describes what he saw with his own eyes, thus expresses himself, and his words may be depended on. "The emperor Alexander, whose character presented a singular compound of liberal views, benevolent intentions, and clear-sighted shrewdness, with an indolent weakness, which allowed him, and consequently his empire, to be entirely governed by his confidants, was perfectly conscious of this rottenness of the social system. As no flattery could make him believe that he was either a Peter the Great or a Napoleon, he never dreamed of undertaking a reform, perhaps the most difficult that had ever been attempted. He was perfectly aware that to have any chance of success, he must begin by raising ten-fold the salaries of his officers, which the finances of the state would not have allowed him, and establishing an unlimited freedom of the press, which his ministers would have considered as the mad act of a political Frankenstein. As he wanted the energy to dispute the matter with his advisers, even when he felt their conduct to be cruel and foresaw it to be impolitic, he never dreamed of removing this mountain of social iniquity; but he at least saw it exactly as it was; and

* Revelations of Russia, Vol. I.

perfectly aware that unless the evil was cured at the root, any severity would prove utterly useless, —a mere film over the ulcer, he allowed corruption to walk barefaced, instead of obliging it, as Nicholas has done, merely to veil itself from the public view. He avenged himself for the public robberies of his servants by a quiet jest, and allowed his ministers to discover, to prove, and to punish. He plainly observed of his Russian subjects: "If they only knew where to warehouse them, they would purloin my line-of-battle ships; if they could do it without waking me, they would steal my teeth while I slept."

Count Stanislaus Plater has endorsed this opinion even more strongly, in a political pamphlet of high reputation.* He says, "There does not exist in Europe, a more immoral system of government; one which, based upon the most shameless venality, has reduced it to a tacit conventional system and habit, which has ceased to shock, and has reached such a pitch, that many persons in Russia cannot conceive it possible for an *employé* to be an honest man. This conviction overwhelmed the last days of the Emperor Alexander with grief and melancholy.

"It was this which excited the imagination of the conspirators in 1825, who, penetrated with the

* Les Polonais au Tribunal de l'Europe.

H 2

sense of the necessity of reform, and dreaming of a better order of things, thought the most frightful overthrow of government preferable to this organised system of corruption. Wherever the Russian government has been introduced, venality has taken root."

Alexander's principal favourite was Count Araktcheieff, a name little known in Europe, but remembered in Russia through every department of the empire. He was not quite as wicked as Potemkin, but he was fully as rapacious. Where his predecessor inflicted the knout, he levied a fine, and instead of banishing political delinquents to Siberia, he squeezed their pockets and kept them at home to fatten up for future exactions. Alexander, who was gentle to weakness, who loved to discuss the rights of humanity, and wept over a tale of sorrow, allowed an unscrupulous minister to tarnish his name by the exercise of oppressions, repugnant to his own nature and foreign to his practice. His constitutional indolence became responsible for the crimes of his delegate. This man, who governed the emperor, and through him the empire, was himself governed by a mistress, a demon in human form, who led him into the most unaccountable excesses, until her career was cut short by assassination at the hand of one of her own slaves.

On the death of Alexander, Araktcheieff fell into disgrace, and retreated on benevolence and reli-. gion when he could no longer exercise political power. He had been faithful to his master, personally unostentatious in his favouritism, and died in 1834, in the odour of sanctity, with his eyes fixed on the portrait of Alexander, suspended in front of his bed.

In 1805, Russia, alarmed at the progress of Napoleon, responded to the cry of Austria in her hour of extremity and came to her assistance— but too late. The capitulation of Ulm, and the surrender of Vienna, were followed up by the crowning disaster of Austerlitz. Alexander was here under fire for the first time. His personal bravery was as conspicuous as the valour of his troops, but he had no Suvaroff to direct their energies, and the Austrian quartermaster-general, Weyrother, who had already lost Rivoli and Hohenlinden by erroneous dispositions, was allowed a third and more decisive opportunity of evincing his incapacity. Koutousoff, the nominal commander-in-chief, fell asleep at the council of war, and had nothing to do with the ill-judged movements which ruined his army. It suited the policy of Napoleon to allow the wrecks of that army to retreat unmolested when they were completely in his power. A second time, Alexander came on to assist Prussia, but again—too late. Prussia was subdued before the armies of the Czar were able to take the field. In the meantime, Russia and Turkey had resumed their old hostilities, and the English government, always intent on the death-struggle with France, with the view of liberating the Russian troops engaged in the East, sought a pretext to quarrel with our old ally the Turk, and sent a fleet up the Dardanelles, under Sir John Duckworth, and an expedition against Alexandria under General Fraser—instances of the " little wars " so detrimental to the credit of a great nation, in which the short-hitting policy of our ministers frequently involved us. Both these armaments came back again with loss and discomfiture. In the meantime Russia maintained a stout campaign in Poland, fought at Pultusk and Eylau with a pertinacity which raised high expectations of a triumphant issue, sank under the genius of Napoleon at Friedland, and was bribed into utter submission at Tilsit, when only half defeated. Alexander then delared war against England, while the balance of her subsidies was yet in his treasury, and he had no other immediate fund from whence to support his armies. History does not present a more flagrant instance of political treachery.

The Treaty of Tilsit was concluded on the 7th July, 1807. The eighth Article provided that " If, in consequence of the recent changes that have occurred at Constantinople (the deposition of Sultan Selim, replaced by Mustapha), the Porte shall not accept the mediation of France, or if, having accepted it, it shall happen that during the course of three months the negotiations are not brought to a satisfactory conclusion, France will make common cause with Russia against the Ottoman Porte, and the two high contracting powers will concert measures to withdraw all the provinces of the Ottoman empire in Europe (Constantinople and the province of Roumelia excepted) from the yoke and vexations of the Turk."

This is plain speaking, divested of circumlocution, but Napoleon soon discovered that if he suffered this project to be literally carried out, the advantages were not on his side. Eventually Russia was permitted to take possession of Finland, as an immediate compromise, and the partition of Turkey was postponed to a more convenient opportunity. The secret stipulations of Tilsit, which purchased the honour of Russia, and tempted the Czar to infringe solemn engagements on flimsy pretexts, never have been and never will be authentically developed in all their details; but enough has transpired to show that the general summary circulated by the English government at the time, was derived from sources to be relied on, and not much exaggerated in design, although few will admit that it was possible of execution.   Here follow the leading stipulations of this most comprehensive and conscientious treaty.*

Article I. Russia shall take possession of European Turkey, and shall extend her conquests into Asia as far as she may deem proper.

Art. II. The Bourbon dynasty in Spain, and the House of Braganza in Portugal, shall cease to reign.   Princes of the family of Napoleon shall succeed to both crowns.

Art. III. The temporal supremacy of the Pope shall cease.   Rome and her dependencies shall be re-united to the kingdom of Italy.

Art. IV. Russia shall afford France the assistance of her navy to re-conquer Gibraltar.

Art. V. France shall take possession of such cities in Africa as Tunis and Algiers, and at the general peace all the conquests made by France

* Bignon, in his " History of French Diplomacy," composed by order of Napoleon, admits the general correctness of this statement; the articles are also given in the " Biographie Universelle " of Michaud.

in Africa shall be given as indemnities to the Kings of Sardinia and Sicily.

Art. VI. Malta shall be held by France, and no peace shall be granted to England till she surrenders that island.

Art. VII. The French shall occupy Egypt.

Art. VIII. The navigation of the Mediterranean shall be confined exclusively to French, Russian, Spanish, and Italian vessels.

Art. IX. Denmark shall have as an indemnity in the north of Europe, the Hanseatic towns, *provided she surrenders her squadrons to France.**

Art. X. Their Majesties the Emperors of France and Russia shall draw up regulations by which no power shall navigate merchant-ships unless possessed of a certain number of vessels of war.

Such a treaty, supposing it could be carried to a consummation, amounts to a division of the world between the two contracting parties. There would not only have been an end of our Indian empire in a year or two, but England would have disappeared from the map of Europe, as an independent nation, within a quarter of a century.

* This clause was anticipated by the British expedition to Copenhagen in Sept., 1807, when the entire Danish fleet was taken and carri·d to England. This time it was not a " little war," but the wisest measure of precaution ever adopted under peculiar circumstances. *O si sic omnia!*

Napoleon was too sagacious to believe in this, but he wanted to impel Alexander into the Continental system, and mystified him accordingly, to render him a subservient instrument. As far as the French Emperor was concerned we had nothing to complain of. It was war to the knife between the two governments, war undisguised and declared, and each had an undoubted right to use every possible means to cripple the opposing enemy. As Conrad the Corsair says of Seyd the Pacha:—

> " He was mine enemy, and swept my band
> From earth with ruthless, but with open hand,
> And therefore came I in my bark of war
> To smite the smiter with the scimitar."

It was not so in the practice of Alexander of Russia. When he lent himself to this secret negotiation, this modern duumvirate, he was at peace with England, without an excuse for complaint or remonstrance, receiving aid and supplies from the power he thus secretly conspired to destroy. The Treaty of Tilsit, with the unpublished codicils, was concluded on the 7th of July; it was not until the 26th of October following that the Emperor of Russia began to talk of reviving the principles of the armed neutrality, threatened to break off communications with England unless the Danish navy should be

restored, and the empire of the seas renounced;
and finally declared war on the 1st of December.
Retribution fell on him before the close of a year.
His trade was speedily annihilated by the English
cruisers, he was enclosed within the gates of the
Baltic, and his squadron in the Tagus, surrendering to Sir C. Cotton, shifted their quarters to
England, where they remained until the close of
the war, rotting in undisturbed neglect under the
old walls of Porchester Castle.

In 1812 we forgot all this, and when Russia
was threatened with invasion, once more extended to her the right hand of friendship, and
again poured forth our subsidies to keep her
armies in the field. As usual, she was late,
even in her own defence, and when Napoleon
crossed the Niemen, had no adequate force to
face and retard him. Much has been said and
written on the organized plan of retreat to draw
the enemy on into the interior, and to insulate
him from his base of operations. Lord Wellington's successful defence of Portugal and the lines
of Torres Vedras, were said to have furnished the
Russian generals with their plan of campaign, of
which the burning of Moscow was a pre-calculated
episode. These are opinions delivered after the
event, and contrived to make causes and consequences cohere, rather than the result of deep-

laid schemes by which the event was produced.
To the astonishment of all Europe, Russia was at
this most momentous crisis later and more ill-
prepared than usual. She retreated because she
had not sufficient force to make a stand; and
when she finally fought at Borodino, did it to
save her capital, which fell as a result of the
battle. The Emperor Alexander, suddenly smit-
ten with the thirst of military glory, so opposite
to his natural temperament, had determined to
take the active command of his own armies, and
was with difficulty dissuaded from this ruinous
intention. Then the commanding generals were
hastily appointed, had no confidence in each
other, and no longer time to arrange connected
operations, even if they had possessed the experience and capacity which the crisis demanded.

The Emperor Nicholas has lately, on more than
one occasion, indecently set forward the triumph
of Russia over the legions of Napoleon in 1812,
which he loudly vaunts as the result of national
prowess and inexhaustible resources. The assump-
tion is merely offensive, without convincing the
most careless reasoners, or the most superficial
observers. It is true, that the result saw Russian
armies marching through the streets of Paris;
but they were brought there by English money.
The two hundred thousand gallant Frenchmen,

whose bones whitened on the steppes of Russia, were victims of the climate rather than the conqueror's sword; the obstinacy of Napoleon created his own disasters; and the active diplomacy of England, seconding Russian intrigues, enabled the Emperor Alexander to make an advantageous peace with Turkey, and to set at liberty a large well-disciplined army at the moment, and in the position where they were most available. The blindness of Turkey in yielding, when the tide was beginning to turn in her favour, is one of those unaccountable events in the history of nations which we pause on and ponder over without being able to comprehend. But the Turks were probably discouraged by repeated defeats, had no longer the means of continuing an active war, and were still further weakened by treachery in their own cabinet. We have already seen that Bessarabia was swindled from them under false pretences.

By the treaty of Bucharest in 1812, Russia advanced her frontier towards Constantinople from the Dniester to the Pruth, a point behind which she has never since receded. She secured for her vessels of war the right of ascending as far as the mouth of the Pruth, and the entire navigation of the Danube for her merchant ships. She obtained an amnesty for the Servians whom she had excited to rebellion against their lawful suzerain; stipulated for the demolition of the Turkish fortresses in Servia; and bound the Porte to mediate a peace with Persia, Russia not being for the moment at liberty to prosecute that war.

The emperor of Russia, on his part, agreed to surrender Anapa, and certain other fortified places on the Asiatic coast of the Black Sea, which had been captured during the war; but the stipulation was not fulfilled; and the bad faith displayed in evading it, became one of the causes of dissension which, in the end, led to another contest.*

All the struggles between Russia and Turkey, since the reign of Peter the Great, have ended in the loss of power and territory to the latter; and, in all, she has been unjustly attacked without provocation. Yet the integrity of Turkish independence has been always admitted as indispensable to the balance of power, while the leading cabinets, who proclaim the principle, have seldom interfered except to overthrow it. Navarino and the kingdom of Greece are evidences to attest this paradox. But it is never too late

* See "Progress and Present Position of Russia in the East," p. 74.

to amend an error, or to prevent the Sultan from crying again, with justice, " Save me from my friends !"

On the 1st of December, 1824, the Emperor of all the Russias died at Taganrog, on the Sea of Azof. He had gone there for the recovery of the empress, little expecting that he was destined to precede her to the tomb. Not many months before, General Diebitsch discovered a conspiracy, which had been brooding for years, involving in its contemplated object the assassination of the monarch, the subversion of the government, and the total revolution of the empire. It began by the establishment of secret societies in the army, spread rapidly amongst the nobility, and even infected the lower classes. Alexander had created great discontent by his indolence in allowing petitions to accumulate in heaps in his cabinet, without even breaking their seals. It was strange, that in a country, where a foreign visitor cannot change his shirt or his coat, or pull off his boots and put on a pair of shoes, without every trifling movement being made the subject of a police report, a plot of many ramifications, and in which thousands were implicated, should remain for years without notice or suspicion; that no treachery should betray, and no loyalty fathom, the impending mischief. The first hint of its exist-

ence came from an inferior officer of Lancers named
Sherwood, and of English origin. He received
for recompense the honour of hereditary nobility,
with the surname of " *Vernei*," the Faithful; but
he did not long enjoy the distinctions conferred
upon him. At the first opening of the campaign
on the Danube in 1828, a ball terminated his
career; but whether from a Russian or a Turkish
musquet is a question which can never be decided.
The knowledge of this plot deeply affected the
mind and spirits of the emperor, already much
depressed by the successive deaths of his children,
legitimate and illegitimate. He knew that he was
marked out for the assassin's dagger; that all the
parts in the tragic drama were assigned; and that
the period of the catastrophe was determined.
His wife appeared to be dying before his eyes;
and, in that moment of depression, all his long
neglect was forgotten, his early affection returned
in full force, and he resolved to devote his life
to her for the future. A chronic malady of the
chest rendered a milder climate absolutely necessary for her recovery. The physicians recommended her native air; but she refused peremp·
torily to comply with this advice, urging in reply
to all representations, that the wife of the Emperor of Russia should die nowhere else than in
his dominions. The Crimea was at first proposed;

but Taganrog was finally fixed upon; and Alexander declared that he would accompany her. He was suffering under a recent attack of erysipelas; but neither he nor his physicians imagined that any danger threatened him, or that the exertion of a journey would bring back his complaint. When assailed by typhus fever, he rejected the proposed remedies, and trusted to the strength of his constitution. The unexpected suddenness of his death, the great distance from the capital at which it occurred, the explosion of the conspiracy almost immediately after, the certainty that his assassination was intended, and would have taken place had he not been removed in the course of nature, the popular belief that Emperors of Russia seldom die in their beds,—these, and other cohering circumstances, occasioned a general impression through Europe, that Alexander had shared the fate of his father, his grandfather, and of other princes of his dynasty. The evidences to the contrary are too convincing to be disputed. The published report of his physician, Sir James Wylie, the letter of the Empress to his mother, and the documents collected by M. Schnitzler in his "Secret History," are more than sufficient to convince all, except those stubborn disputants who are predetermined to reject conviction on the most unde-

I

niablè proof. The Empress Elizabeth followed her
husband to the grave at the expiration of five months.

On the decease of Alexander, the crown belonged incontestably to the Grand Duke Constantine, his next brother, although he had never
been publicly designated as heir - presumptive.
The question had never arisen during the reign
of the late monarch. In the event of the death
of the Empress Elizabeth, Alexander might marry
again, and givè a direct heir to the throne. But
now he was dead, and that was no longer possible.
The act of Paul, regulating the succession, had
been confirmed by Alexander in 1807 and again
in 1820. In this last, he also decreed that the
issue of marriages recognized and authorized by
the reigning emperor, and who should themselves
contract marriages recognized and authorised by
him, should alone enjoy that right of succession
to the throne which had been established by Paul.
Nothing could be more complete, more rational,
or more clear than this law. It existed, moreover, in full force and vigour. Constantine was universally unpopular. A gallant soldier from his
early youth, he had fought in many battles, and
had invariably distinguished himself by the most
daring valour. He received the title of Czarovitch
from his father Paul for his bravery in Italy
with Suvaroff, while yet under twenty - one

years of age. At Austerlitz, in 1805, he led the
Imperial Guard into the thickest of the fight, and
had two horses shot under him. At Pultusk,
Eylau, and Friedland, he was equally distinguished;
but still the army, though they admired his
courage and followed him to death, had no respect
for his person, no attachment to the individual
man. He was feared and obeyed, from instinct
and habit—not from impulse or affection. He
was known to possess an ungovernable temper, a
cruel disposition, a memory tenacious of wrongs,
and a heart incapable of friendship. In aspect he
was, if possible, more forbidding than his father,
with the same Calmuck features, the stunted nose,
the shaggy eyebrows, and the protruding lip.
When men looked on him, they felt as if they
saw an ogre or a ghoul. When he looked on men,
they shrank as if under the influence of the "evil
eye," and endured a sickness of the heart until
the glance wandered away to settle on another
object. He was even more repulsive in mirth
than in anger. While describing an imaginary
being, the poet has typified him in these expres-
sive lines :—

> " There was a laughing devil in his sneer,
>   That raised emotions both of rage and fear;
>   And where his frown of hatred darkly fell,
>   Hope withering fled, and mercy sigh'd farewell !" *

* Lord Byron's " Corsair," Canto I.

The multitude entertained no doubt that at the death of Alexander the imperial crown would be worn by Constantine, and the pulse of fifty-eight millions trembled with apprehension. The miseries of the reign of Paul rose again before them in visions of fearful anticipation. Yet Constantine has found his panegyrists, as Nero had his mourners. They have said that although his temper was diabolical, his heart was good; and that as often as he committed fearful outrages under the influence of passion, he repented when he became cool. This sort of posthumous atonement was of little value to the victims he had sacrificed, and no security to the survivors, who hourly expected a repetition of the wrong, but were by no means so confident in the accompanying apology.

When Alexander was supposed to be seriously ill in 1824, Constantine suddenly appeared in St. Petersburgh. The inhabitants were unable to disguise the terror with which they looked forward to his probable accession, and nothing could exceed the joy of all classes, on the temporary recovery of their beloved sovereign. During the last illness of Alexander, bulletins of his health were sent direct from Taganrog to the Grand Duke Constantine at Warsaw, with as much diligence as those to the Empress-Mother at St.

Petersburgh, and he received the first information of the event which threw the empire into mourning. The brother or the heir might have equally expected these communications, yet the constant despatch of couriers confirmed the general belief with regard to the intended succession. Constantine had no children by his first wife, the Princess Julienne of Saxe - Cobourg, sister of Leopold, King of Belgium. They separated by mutual consent at the end of four years. After many scruples and much delay, Alexander connived at his second marriage with Jeanne Gudzinska, a Polish lady, of whom he was deeply enamoured, and who retained her magical influence over his savage temper until the hour of his death. Whatever he might have been to others, to her he was kind and affectionate, and her society became necessary to his existence. The union was what is termed in courtly phraseology, morganatic or left-handed. The parties were united in wedlock, but their posterity (if they had any) could have no claim to the succession.

Nicholas was many years younger than Constantine, and it appeared highly probable that he would ultimately be emperor, but only after the demise of his elder brother, whose personal right had in no way been compromised by his first divorce or his second marriage. Jeanne Gudzinska, created

Princess of Lowicz by Alexander, deserves to be mentioned with respect. The woman who could soften and almost transform a character so ferocious and ungovernable as that of Constantine, must have been herself truly amiable. Her influence principally prevailed on him to renounce the throne, his occupation of which would have produced the misery of millions, ending in sanguinary revolution; and by personal ascendancy she taught him self-control, and obtained from him the tenderness of a lover to the hour of his death. She survived him only a few months, and died at St. Petersburgh on the 29th of November, 1831.

As soon as the news of the death of Alexander arrived at St. Petersburgh, the Grand Duke Nicholas repaired to the senate to take the oath of fidelity to his brother Constantine (then at Warsaw), as " the legitimate heir to the empire by right of primogeniture," and to issue a command to the whole empire to follow his example. But a document had been deposited with the senate, on which was written in Alexander's hand, "In the event of my death, this packet to be opened at an extraordinary sitting, before proceeding to any other business." The packet was opened, and found to contain the voluntary renunciation of his right to the succession by Constantine, dated 26th of January, 1822, ratified by Alexander on the 14th of February following, and a declaration that the Grand Duke Nicholas, his second brother, was thenceforward to be considered as his heir. It appears certain, on a comparison of evidence, and weighing all the circumstances of the case, that Nicholas was quite aware of the existence of this document, and of the abdication of Constantine;—that his first public act was one of intentional, studied duplicity, the reasons for which he will never explain until summoned to answer before the awful tribunal to which earthly sovereigns are alone responsible.

The high council of the state, in obedience to the commands of Alexander, proceeded to take the oath of fidelity to the hereditary emperor he had named; but Nicholas declined receiving the proffered homage, and refused to assume the sovereign power, unless his elder brother persisted in the renunciation of his rights. Was he sincere, or was he acting a part, having previously calculated the certain result? An obstinate altercation ensued between the bashful autocrat and the council. At last the latter extricated themselves by a compromise. "You are our Emperor," they said; "we owe you absolute obedience. If you order us to recognize the

Grand Duke Constantine as our legitimate sovereign, our course is to obey your commands."

Constantine was then proclaimed; the ministers
of the Church assented; the army cried, "Glory
to God!" and the people looked on, knowing
there was a change, and not caring much about
the matter. The motives by which Nicholas may
have been actuated were many and various, according to the interpretations given by himself,
his friends, and his enemies. These must be
weighed, and a decision formed according to their
comparative value.

Constantine, by the act of Nicholas, was virtually Emperor, and a dangerous interregnum
ensued, which might very easily have led to a
revolution. There was everywhere the ominous
silence of suspense, the journals were mute,
people looked on each other without speaking,
and grief for the death of Alexander seemed to
be the prevailing sentiment: the future was un-
heeded in the present. Constantine settled the
difficulty, and relieved the embarrassment of all
concerned by peremptorily refusing the crown,
and adhering to the tenor of his renunciation.
There was now no reason for further delay or
hesitation.

An interregnum of three weeks terminated on
the 24th of December, and Nicholas ascended the

throne, which he knew to be his, from the moment that the death of Alexander was announced. He dates his accession from the 1st of December, 1825, the day on which Alexander died; but his reign did not in reality commence until the 24th, when the manifesto was signed, though not made public. The act was short, clear, and drawn up with remarkable ability.

The advent of Nicholas to the throne was the signal for the breaking-out of the long organized conspiracy, the heads of which in St. Petersburgh were Sergius, Prince Troubetskoi; Eugene, Prince Nolenski; and Conrad Ryleieff. The latter, less rich, lower in rank, and inferior in influence, possessed the superior qualities of firmness and prudence. He was a poet, an enthusiast, a democrat, and a man of theories. They had long determined to get rid of Alexander, and subvert the government. The succession of Nicholas hastened their plans to the moment of decisive action. On the 25th of December, Christmas Day, the conspirators met for the last time at the house of Ryleieff, to concert their final measures. It is said that the police were apprised of this meeting, and gave information of it to the Governor-General of St. Petersburgh, Count Miloradovitch, who only laughed, crying "Bah! they are a set of dreamers, met to read bad verses!" Nicholas had been made acquainted with the existence of the conspiracy, but seemed to treat it as a thing of nought. The conspirators, in the meantime, had been misled by an assurance, that in the second army one hundred thousand men were ready to declare for them. The revolt broke out in the regiment of Moscow, and when Nicholas issued from the Winter Palace to suppress it, he was uncertain what battalions were faithful, or what would declare against him. Many cried " Long live Constantine!" but he soon found himself surrounded by soldiers and generals constant in fidelity, and more numerous than their opponents.

In this momentous crisis, and at the very opening of his reign, he was suddenly called upon to exhibit himself worthy of the throne by courage and moderation, and it must be admitted that he displayed both in admirably blended proportions. His faithful friend Miloradovitch, who had escaped from fifty-six battles with foreign enemies without a wound, and who had been called the Murat of the Russian army, fell by his side, and by the hand of one of his own soldiers. The mob, assembled in large numbers, began to take part with the armed rebels. The Emperor, deeply grieved by the fall of Miloradovitch, was now sufficiently reinforced, but still he hesitated before he wielded the vast power in his hands, and issued orders to shed the blood of his subjects. He tried exhortations, but they refused to listen. The pontiff Seraphim appeared and appealed to them in the name of their religion, but they received his discourse with scoffs, and stifled his voice by the rolling of the drums. It was now absolutely necessary to act. The cavalry charged, but the rebels resisted stoutly, and the short winter's day had nearly closed in darkness before the conflict was decided. Field-pieces were at length brought into action, and a general rout took place. The exact loss has never been ascertained. The bodies were hastily collected and thrown into the Neva, through openings hewn for the purpose in the ice. There might have been in all some two hundred killed, and from seven to eight hundred taken prisoners. At six o'clock all was quiet. The Emperor hastened to re-assure the Empress, and then hurried to the dying bed of Miloradovitch, to receive his last wishes, and thank him for the final service he had rendered to his country at the price of his blood. The conspiracy was over, and the leaders who had excited it were found wanting in the hour of danger. True to the traditional character of demagogues, they had brought their excited dupes to the field and left them there to perish. But they were hunted out by the police, and cast into prison.

The subsequent executions were few,* and the
clemency of Nicholas raised the most exalted
hopes of his future justice in the administration of
the great empire which had submitted unanimously and cheerfully to his rule. Why have
the consummate prudence and admirable moderation which marked the conduct of Nicholas in
the early vigour of life, so signally deserted him
in its decline, and when advancing years should
bring with them increasing wisdom? We cannot
solve the enigma, but we see in the present conduct of the Russian Emperor another instance of
the strange inconsistency which so often mars
the characters of sovereigns, who have been
quoted up to a certain point as models of political
experience and practical wisdom. We have beheld
a memorable instance in the fall of Louis Philippe,
and perhaps Nicholas is destined to furnish a

* Troubetskoi, who deserved compound execution for his
blended treason, cowardice, and ignorance; who talked of
Brutus and Riego, but confessed that he knew not who those
patriots were—Troubetskoi was spared, and banished to
Siberia for life. Ryleieff and four others were hanged. The
platform was withdrawn before its time, and the noose slid
over the head of Ryleieff, with two of his companions, precipi-
tating them into the hole beneath the scaffold. When they
were once more brought under the gibbet, Ryleieff exclaimed
with undaunted courage: "Accursed country, where they
neither know how to plot, to judge, or to hang!" Such a high-
souled spirit should have fallen by a bullet on the day of the
insurrection, instead of surviving to perish ignominiously by
the halter.

second, and if possible a more impressive illustration. Ambition is usually an accompaniment of youth and hot blood, a desire which grows with indulgence, and becomes stunted by restraint. In him, after long forbearance, this overwhelming influence bursts forth in the autumn of life, at the mature age of fifty-eight, a period when the active, stormy passions are usually exhausted by indulgence and sobered by reflection. He has gone through a long series of difficulty and trial, and severe discipline has been administered to him in his greatness. His reign was inaugurated by bloodshed, and seven years later he was induced to put down the revolt of Poland by sanguinary retaliation. His cities have been destroyed by fire, famine and the cholera have decimated his provinces, his domestic circle has been reached by the keen arrows of death, and now he stands alone unnecessarily braving the indignation of the world, rushing madly into an unequal contest which he has most unnecessarily provoked, and from which it is not humanly probable that he can escape without signal disaster and humiliation.

From the close of the great war in 1815 to the accession of the Emperor Nicholas, only ten years had elapsed; during which time, Russia, in common with the other nations, was occupied in recruiting her exhausted strength. She was in no state for immediate aggression, but had contrived to take good care of herself at the settlement of states by the Congress of Vienna. France lost her conquests, England resigned many colonies and desirable outports, but Russia was called upon to give up nothing. Finland, all her acquisitions in Turkey and Persia, were recognized as hers, and a proposition to restore Poland was peremptorily negatived by the plundering partitioners. Turkey was passed over as of no moment, although the necessity of preserving her independence was admitted as a maxim in all arguments and negotiations. Russia in a short time began to stir, and having excited the revolt in the Morea, offered her aid to the Porte to put it down. She had previously signed a treaty in conjunction with France and England, binding her to unite with the Western Powers in settling the affairs of Greece; and some months after entered into another convention with Turkey, by which she expressly agreed to abstain from all interference. By some flagrant political mistakes of his own, and more by a long tissue of political double-dealing on the part of his supposed friends, but actual enemies, the unfortunate Sultan Mahmoud found himself driven into a war with the three most powerful nations of the world, and without an ally except his then loyal vassal of Egypt.

As soon as Nicholas was firmly seated on his throne, a short time sufficed to put down plots, to dissipate intended insurrections, and to restore public tranquillity through the vast provinces of the Russian Empire. Early in 1828 he was ready to resume the suspended march to Constantinople, and accordingly his armies once more inundated the frontier principalities, those unhappy debatable lands, which Russia alternately seizes and abandons to seize again, and which the northern bear never fails to pounce upon just as they are beginning to recover blood and sinew, and to swell a little from the last merciless squeezing. Unhappy is the destiny of small states, geographically placed between greater ones who are always quarrelling, and have no other highway by which to rush into mutual conflict. If they look to the right, they find plunder and protection; if to the left, protection and plunder. They are worse off than the border lands of England and Scotland under the old feudal quarrels, when the Douglas and the Percy were perpetually exercising their rival chivalry, or a penniless chieftain found it necessary to replenish his larder or his wine-cellar.

The ostensible Russian pretext against Turkey,

was then, as now, the religious obligation by
which the Emperor felt himself imperatively
called upon to rescue his suffering brothers in
the faith. The Sultan was worse prepared than
ever; Greece was in open rebellion, and on the
verge of independence; by a fatal mistake we
had destroyed his fleet, and that of his Egyptian
ally at Navarino; and he himself had extirpated
the old indigenous soldiers of the empire, the
janissaries, while his new levies, modelled on a
foreign plan, were raw and ineffective. The
fiery, enthusiastic valour of Asia had been driven
out, but the sustained discipline of Europe was
not yet imported. Nevertheless he made a
gallant resistance against the leviathan, and at
the end of the first year his adversaries had little
to boast of. They had taken Ibraila by capitulation, and Varna by treachery, but retreated from
before the lines of Schumla, and raised the siege
of Silistria. In the mean time, Paskievitch
pressed rapidly on the Asiatic side; took Erivan
and Erzeroum, threatened Trebizond, and advanced into Anatolia. The Sultan left his
capital, bearing the sacred standard, but the
last appeal failed to excite the national enthusiasm that was expected. Diebitsch crossed the
Balkan with forty thousand men, abandoned his
base of operations, and entered Adrianople.

Then the Sultan Mahmoud was terrified into peace, which he concluded on the 14th of September, 1829, on terms almost amounting to the dismemberment of his empire. The successes of Paskievitch alarmed him as much as the advance of Diebitsch. When we remember the overwhelming odds against which he obstinately fought, it is marvellous that he was enabled to resist so long.

" By this Treaty of Adrianople," says the author of " Russia in the East," " the Emperor Nicholas, who in deference to the jealousy of Europe had publicly disclaimed all intentions to aggrandize his dominions, acquired Anapa and Poti, with a considerable extent of coast on the Black Sea, a portion of the pashalic of Akhilska, with the two fortresses of Akhilska and Akhilkillak, and the virtual possession of the islands formed by the mouths of the Danube; stipulated for the destruction of the Turkish fortress of Giurgevo, and the abandonment by Turkey of the right bank of the St. George's branch of the Danube, to the distance of several miles from that river; attempted a virtual separation of Moldavia and Wallachia from Turkey, by sanitary regulations intended to connect them with Russia; stipulated that the Porte should confirm the internal regulations for the government of those

K

provinces which Russia had established while she occupied them; removed, partly by force and partly by the influence of the priesthood, many thousand families of Armenians from the Turkish provinces in Asia to his own territories, as he had already moved nearly an equal number from Persia, leaving whole districts depopulated, and sacrificing, by the fatigues and privations of the compulsory march, the aged and infirm, the weak and the helpless."

As another result of this disastrous war, Greece was declared to be an independent state, under the protection of the great powers of Europe. At the commencement of the struggle it had been proposed to the Sultan that, as in the cases of Moldavia and Wallachia, he should still retain the suzerainty, with a yearly tribute; but he rejected those terms with indignation, and Greece was finally severed from his empire.

Count Capo D'Istria, (a native of Corfu, and the son of a physician,) who had been a Russian minister, was placed at the head of the government with the title of President. He was not long permitted to enjoy his elevation, being assassinated on November 9th, 1831, by the brother and son of Mavromichaelis, a Mainote chief, whom he had imprisoned. Resolved to be classical in all their procedings, the authorities revived for the special punishment of these criminals, the old Bœotian mode of execution by burying alive; a barbarity exercised by Creon in the case of his niece Antigone, sister of Polynices, B.C. 1225. They were sentenced to be immured within brick walls built around them up to their chins, and to be scantily supplied with food under this species of slow torture, until they died. It was then determined to change the new republic into a monarchy; but the throne of Greece had become an unpromising investment, and was some time in the market before a customer could be found.

It has been said that it was seriously offered to the Duke of Wellington, who laughed at the proposal, considering it as an amusing jest; but recommended Prince Leopold, who was then unprovided for, and supposed to be on the look-out for a vacant sovereignty. Leopold coquetted a little, as if tempted by the bauble, but finally proved himself a wise man in his generation, and declined. The snug little kingdom of Belgium which soon afterwards fell in,* though less brilliantly furnished with heroic reminiscences, is more secure, and through his sagacious government, has stood unmoved while continental Europe

* The Duke de Nemours was elected king of Belgium in the first instance, but his father, King Louis Philippe, refused his consent.

was convulsed with revolutions. It had besides, in those unsettled days, the additional advantage of being nearer Claremont in case of accidents.

Otho of Bavaria was declared King of Greece, January 25th, 1833, and has ever been a mere puppet in the hands of subtle Russian diplomatists. Like many wiser men, he is entirely under the influence of his wife, who, it must be remembered, is a princess of the Russian house of Oldenburg. They have no children; and although the succession is fixed is the Bavarian line, the Queen expects to alter it.

The Greeks have their eyes on Constantinople, and undervalue the narrow strip to which they are at present circumscribed. They indulge in a dream that sooner or later the whole Hellenic race will be united into one kingdom; an anticipation of the future cherished under the name of Panhellenism, and firmly believed in throughout the length and breadth of the land. Russia encourages this idea for deep purposes of her own, but has no intention of aiding in its fulfilment, or that Constantinople shall ever be the capital of an independent Greek empire. Her gaze is incessantly fixed on the tempting aspect of the Golden Horn, but she would rather her ancient enemy, the decrepid Ottoman, should remain tenant in possession, on sufferance, of what she has long considered her destined property, than that a new compact state, rising in youthful vigour, and professing the same creed with herself, should step into his place, and thus protract the conquest *sine die.* On the other hand, France and England, while bent on preserving a barrier against the encroachments of Russia, are not likely to unite in thrusting Greece into the slippers of Turkey, although Greece may be anxious enough to figure in them. The independence of Turkey is essential to the political existence of Greece, their commercial relations are reciprocally advantageous, and a good understanding between the two powers will strengthen both. But Russian intrigue will not allow the government of Greece to see this, and is perpetually at work to check the progress of any opinion that tends to extirpate old jealousies, or to promote the oblivion of exaggerated wrongs.

Another heavy burden was imposed on the exhausted finances of Turkey, in 1829, by the imposition of an enormous indemnity, to make good the expenses of the war, and the commercial losses of Russia. The sum was not likely to be liquidated before the lapse of many years, and until payment was completed, Moldavia, Wallachia, and the fortress of Silistria were to remain as pledges in the hands of the conqueror. But the Sultan did contrive to discharge this heavy obligation, and within the stipulated time.

During the Turkish war of 1828, 1829, the Emperor Nicholas took the field in person, accompanied by his brother, the Grand Duke Michael. Both were present in many engagements; but it has never been pretended that either exhibited the slightest military skill, or the talents of a general. Russia, as we have seen, obtained advantages almost amounting to absolute conquest. These advantages cost her the lives of nearly 200,000 men, on which the Emperor never bestowed a second thought. The sword destroyed many, and famine and pestilence more, and one half at least fell victims to the total want of hospital accommodation. The survivors had scarcely reached their own frontiers, when the Polish Revolution broke out on November 29th, 1830, and once more that oppressed nation rose in determined energy to make a last desperate struggle for emancipation. Had this attempt been organized a year or two sooner, while Russia was still engaged in the Turkish war, the result might have been different. Skrzynecki and Dwernicki proved themselves worthy successors of Kosciusko. They won many battles, and always against superior numbers. Growchow, Wawre, Seroczyn, Seidletz, Zelicho, Ostrolenka, and Wilna, are not names which the Russian regiments will inscribe on their standards, or commemorate over their flowing cups if they are ever permitted to indulge in hilarious potations. Diebitsch, "the Balkan-passer," saw his star turn pale on the plains of Poland. He died suddenly June 10th, 1831, whether from poison, chagrin, or fever, has never been clearly determined. Twelve days later, the Grand Duke Constantine followed him, under the same suspicious circumstances. Up to this period the Russian army had been chiefly led by foreigners, in accordance with the well-known bias of the Emperor; but now Paskievitch, an ultra-Russian, assumed the command, and brought the war to a successful conclusion. The Poles, like Pyrrhus of old, had been ruined by their victories: they had no reserves; their resources were exhausted; they became disunited and mistrustful of their leaders; another desperate encounter at Winsk, and a final defeat at Warsaw on the 9th of September, and the struggle was at an end. Overwhelming numbers again prevailed against courage and patriotism. Poland was extinguished, but Russia triumphed without glory.

On the 26th of July, 1832, Nicholas issued an ukase, decreeing that the kingdom of Poland should thenceforward form an integral portion of the Russian Empire. The sanguinary conduct of the war, and the severities exercised when it was ended, he justified to his conscience, as the legitimate exercise of sovereign power over rebellious vassals ; he stood alone in his opinions, and found no sympathy beyond the narrow circle of his immediate flatterers and sycophants. That the restoration of Poland in its full integrity would be an effectual barrier against the present encroachments of Russia, and a guarantee for the future, cannot be disputed. Whether, under any circumstances likely to arise out of the impending war, that is still practicable, is a very doubtful and momentous question for the Western nations to consider.

The Poles have been so long subdued and divided that their nationality is supposed to be extinct. Perhaps it only slumbers : 1854 is not as far from 1830, as the latter date was from 1794; a people who twice looked up towards victory when fighting alone, may grapple it at last if powerfully supported. There are overgrown states, with less claims, which may be stripped of unlawful spoils to secure the independence of Europe, and to consummate an act of retributive justice. The material point is to watch and combine the time and opportunity, which sometimes arise when least expected. The idea may be scouted as chimerical, but many solid realities of the present day were much more imaginative and improbable five years ago. We live in an age of miracles, and have witnessed with our own eyes the accomplishment of events, which exceed the wildest flights of romantic fiction.

Long before .Turkey could recover from the prostrate state to which she had been reduced by the treaty of Adrianople, fresh blows were struck from an unexpected quarter. Mehemet Ali renounced his allegiance, erected Egypt and Syria into an independent kingdom, and advanced boldly to attack and dethrone his lawful sovereign and master. Europe looked on, saw this storm gathering, but neither appreciated the consequences nor the necessity of anticipating them. This principle of fomenting external discord and domestic rebellion was originally promoted by Russia in 1772; it failed then from the avowed arrogance of Alexis Orloff, the favourite of Catherine, but had never been lost sight of, and at length approached consummation in 1832. Ibrahim Pacha, after a series of successes, in which the superiority of the Egyptian troops over those of the Sultan was invariably established, marched on to within eighty leagues of Constantinople; and there no longer existed any opposing force

to stay his progress until he dictated terms opposite to the walls of the Seraglio. In this campaign the son of Mehemet Ali proved himself a
good general, and conducted his operations with
prudence, sagacity, and vigour. On the other
hand the Turkish commanders opposed to him
were utterly ignorant of their business, and knew
not how to handle troops in action. These troops
were bad, but the Egyptians were not much
better; it was a contest between the one-eyed
and the blind, as Frederick the Great said of the
early battles between the Turks and Russians.
Ibrahim was fortunate in an able second : Suliman
Pacha (otherwise Colonel Selves), who held the
important post of chief of the Egyptian staff, or
as we may call him, quartermaster-general, had
been a field officer in the French army, and
aide-de-camp to Marshal Ney, during the brilliant
wars of the Empire. Marshal Marmont has said,
that although he then filled merely a subordinate
station, he had acquired as thorough a knowledge
of the great principles of the art of war as if he
had served in the highest rank.

In his last extremity the Sultan Mahmoud
applied for foreign aid against his revolted vassal.
It is quite certain that his first appeal was made
to England, his second to France; but neither of
these countries was at that moment disposed or

prepared to respond. In despair, and most re-, luctantly, he threw himself into the arms of Russia, who eagerly embraced the opportunity which she had assisted to create, came down at once with a powerful fleet and army, and Ibrahim Pacha was compelled to retire.

To the astonishment of all the world, Russia also retired when her friendly mission was accomplished, and apparently without asking any fee or reward for the timely rescue. She even restored Silistria to the Sultan unasked, and as a graceful tribute of acknowledgment for his punctilious observance of the treaty of Adrianople. But it soon transpired that a new treaty had been signed at Unkiar-Skelessi, containing a secret article, which virtually accomplished the long-cherished schemes of Russia, and reduced the Porte to the condition of a tributary.

The general stipulations of this treaty engage the two contracting parties to afford mutual aid against mutual enemies; but by the secret article, Turkey, in place of military assistance to Russia, bound herself to close the Bosphorus and the Dardanelles, when called upon to do so by her ally, against the ships of war of all other nations. The right of Turkey to exercise this exclusion as a common principle, without reserve, had never been questioned, neither were the maritime nations of Europe desirous to take from her the control of her own waters; but they never contemplated or intended to allow the dictatorial usupation of that privilege by Russia; or that Russia should command Turkey to exercise it, whenever she herself might happen to be at war with any naval power. It was perfectly evident that by this secret understanding Russia constituted herself viceroy over the Sultan, and became *protector* of the state, which in her regular course of practice she would proceed to annex with the first convenient opportunity. Many steps towards the ultimate object were gained without any overt act to excite the immediate suspicion of other nations, who were at the moment sufficiently occupied with their own domestic affairs. It would have been diametrically opposed to the projects of Russia to suffer Egypt to take the place of Turkey, or to allow a new Mohammedan empire to erect itself on the ruins of the old one.

When the conditions of this treaty transpired in due time, the French and English governments detected the hidden mischief through the apparent plausibility; they not only expressed at once their dissatisfaction, but distinctly signified that they should disregard the stipulation whenever the course of events might render such a course desirable. The French Chargé d'Affaires at St.

Petersburgh, M. de Lagrené, addressed an official
note to Count Nesselrode, the Russian Minister
for Foreign Affairs, in which he clearly stated
that the treaty of the 8th July, 1833, in the
opinion of the French monarch, imparted to the
mutual relations of the Ottoman and Russian
empires, a new character, against which all the
powers of Europe had a right to protest. He
also added, in most unequivocal terms, that if
the articles of that treaty were hereafter to bring
on an armed intervention of Russia in the internal affairs of Turkey, the government of King
Louis Philippe would hold itself wholly at liberty
to adopt such a line of conduct as circumstances
might suggest, acting from that moment as if
the said treaty was a nullity and had no existence ;
a plain announcement, which it was impossible to
misunderstand. Count Nesselrode replied, that
as the French government had merely stated
regret and objections to the treaty of Unkiar-
Skelessi, without explaining the motives or nature
of either, he could neither know nor understand
what was intended. The treaty, according to his
interpretation, was exclusively *defensive ;* it had
been concluded between two independent powers,
exercising their undoubted rights, and containing
nothing prejudicial to the interests of any other
state whatever. If these states were determined

to set it aside as of no value, it was clear they had in view the subversion of an empire which the treaty was destined to preserve. The act had indeed changed the nature of the relations between Russia and the Porte; for it had produced confidence and close intimacy in place of long-cherished mistrust, and had moreover given to the Turkish government a guarantee of stability with a means of defence calculated to ensure its preservation. He then concluded, by informing the French ambassador, that His Majesty the Emperor, his august master, was resolved to fulfil faithfully, should the occasion present itself, each and all of the obligations which the treaty of the 8th of July imposed upon him, acting therein as if the declaration contained in M. de Lagrené's note did not exist.

In this skirmish of diplomacy the course adopted by France was prompt and spirited, while the reply of Count Nesselrode is imperious even to insolence, and hypocritical to absurdity. The correspondence means defiance on either side, and resembles that recorded to have taken place between two neighbouring kings of old, one of whom addressed the other thus: " Send me your tribute, or else——;" to which he received for answer, " I owe you no tribute, and if——."

The remonstrance of the English cabinet, with

the corresponding reply, we have not access to, but, entertaining exactly the same views with those expressed by France, there can be no doubt that it was equally explicit, and subsequent events have shown that both governments disregarded the empty prohibition, and despatched their fleets through the Dardanelles and the Bosphorus to the Black Sea, when they deemed it necessary to to do so, in utter contempt of the autocratic *veto*, which exercised no real power beyond the limits of the parchment on which it was inscribed.

Sultan Mahmoud died on the 27th June, 1839; his death being supposed to be accelerated by indulgences not in strict accordance with the tenets of the Koran. After his decease, the cellars of the imperial palace were found to be well stored with claret, champagne, and (*proh pudor!*) even with brandy, which his successor, with holy abhorrence, banished from their unseemly resting-places. The Turks had a superstitious conviction that Mahmoud was destined to be the last of their emperors that should reign in Europe. The conquest obtained by his ancestor they believed destined to be lost again by a descendant of the same name, and in him the realization of the prophecy was expected. In like manner the Russians expect that as a Constantine was the last Christian monarch of the eastern empire, a Constantine is to be the next; and point to the Grand Duke, the second son of the Emperor Nicholas, as the destined restorer. This young prince, born on the 21st September, 1827, and grand-admiral of Russia, is said to possess energetic ability, and the characteristic ambition of his race. His elder brother, Alexander, heir-presumptive to the throne, has been described as mild in disposition, limited in talent, and fearful of responsibility. "What makes you so serious?" said Constantine, one day, observing him in profound meditation, with a desponding aspect. "I am thinking of what may be reserved for me in future," replied Alexander; "the charge of ruling an enormous empire is heavy indeed." The younger brother quickly rejoined, "If there is nothing else to torment you, speak the word, and I will instantly relieve you of that same charge."*

The Grand Duke Alexander was born in 1818; he is consequently now in his thirty-sixth year. In 1839, he married a princess of Hesse-Darmstadt, and has several children. Constantine espoused, in 1848, a daughter of the Duke of Saxe-Altenberg, and has also a young family; there are two more brothers, Nicholas and Michael. It will be observed, that the sons of the reigning

* See Schnitzler's "Secret History."

emperor have received the same names as the sons of Paul, and in the same order. The line of Romanoff is at present well represented by male descendants, although accruing through the female branch, and is in no danger of extinction from natural decay. Russian aggrandizement has seldom exhibited itself in ambitious alliances. The present Empress, sister of the King of Prussia, is more highly connected than any of her predecessors on the throne.

The Sultan Mahmoud was the most unfortunate of reformers. Far in advance of his people, he endeavoured to bring them up to his own standard, but his efforts were beyond his resources, and recoiled on himself. They shook his tottering empire to the verge of dissolution. Mehemet Ali of Egypt, another eminent reformer, more unscrupulous than Mahmoud, with limited means and unpromising materials to work with, met with greater success, and contrived to erect a strong kingdom out of a weak vice-royalty. The death of Mahmoud left the throne to his son Abd-ul-Medjid, the present Sultan, at that time a mere youth, of undeveloped character, a sickly constitution, and the last male representative of the line of Othman. The opportunity was tempting, and once more the Egyptian vassal thought to trample on his master. The Turkish

L

fleet sent from Constantinople to coerce him, was
treacherously delivered into his hands, and Ibrahim Pacha prepared confidently to repeat the
marches and victories of 1832, with a more decisive result.   In this fresh danger, the Porte was
again saved, principally by the active interference
of England : France, being offended, stood aloof.
Russian armies were not called in, and Austria
acted as a nominal ally, with two or three small
ships to represent her pretensions as a naval
power.   The capture of Sidon, the defeat at Bey-
rout, and the destruction of Acre, followed in
rapid succession, and convinced Ibrahim and his
father, that their dream of sitting on the throne of
the Ottomans was dissipated for ever. After much
expostulation, the Sultan was finally prevailed upon
by the four powers, England, Austria, Russia,
and Prussia to declare the pachalic of Egypt
hereditary in the family of Mehemet Ali, who
then evacuated Syria, and restored the Turkish
fleet.   France was conciliated by this result,
which promised peace to the East, and seemed to
reassure the continuance of Turkey amongst the
great independent nations of Europe.   Much
diplomatic chicanery was put in practice by Russia, to preserve the undue ascendancy she had
acquired by the surreptitious treaty of Unkiar
Skelessi.   The English government, who the-

roughly fathomed the designs of the Czar, was determined not to be imposed on. The success of Admiral Stopford and Commodore Napier had laid bare the real weakness of Mehemet Ali, and the moral superiority of the Sultan, whose authority had been vindicated for once, without appealing to the active interposition of Russia. Russia felt that France totally disbelieved, and England mistrusted her. She therefore made a merit of yielding what she found it impossible to retain, and regained for the moment the confidence of England, while France was pushed out of the negotiation, in which she had never desired to be a participator, and declined signing the new treaty of London, concluded on the 15th July, 1840.

By this treaty, the four contracting powers, "animated by the desire of maintaining the integrity and independence of the Ottoman Empire, *as a security for the peace of Europe,*" engaged to compel Mehemet Ali, by force of arms, to confine himself for the future within his pachalic of Egypt. The forces they might employ, were to be sent on the demand of the Sultan, and to be withdrawn when he no longer required their presence. The ancient privilege of Turkey to refuse entrance into the Dardanelles and Bosphorus, to the ships of war of foreign nations, was recognized and solemnly pledged to be maintained. The Sultan, on his part, undertook to act on this principle, as the established rule of the empire, *as long as the Porte is at peace.* The command of the straits was thus distinctly restored to Turkey, the secret article of Unkiar Skelessi was nullified, and the friendly alliance of the four powers substituted for the insidious and exclusive protection of Russia.

The cause of offence given by Russia to France was one not likely to be soon forgotten by a high-spirited people. The northern autocrat detested the revolution of 1830, and looked with personal contempt on the citizen-king, whom the French people had chosen to place upon their throne. The Emperor Nicholas talked idly of interposition by force of arms, to restore the exiled dynasty, while he used the safer weapons of intrigue with ready activity. England, taking a sounder view of the policy by which the civilization of the world is to be advanced, regretted the estrangement of France, on a question so important as the affairs of the East. The British government therefore, admitting and acting to the fullest extent on the doctrine, that all nations have an undoubted right to settle their domestic arrangements, without consulting the feelings or opinions of foreign powers, laboured incessantly

to bring France within the circle of the new convention. The designs of Russia, with which all the
world were fully impressed, could never be effectually controlled, while a great military state
remained undecided in her intentions.

On the 13th July, 1841, the existing impediments were removed, the efforts of the English
ministers were crowned with success; and a fresh
treaty announced, that France had joined with
the other leading powers of Europe, in acknow-
ledging the sovereign rights of the Sultan, and in
a solemn league and covenant, to assist him in
consolidating the repose of his Empire. Unless
it could be proved that Turkey cancelled this
engagement by an act of suicidal aggression, any
attempt on the part of one of the contracting
guardians of peace, to trench upon the rights
which all were equally bound to maintain, was to
be considered as a manifest breach of faith, and a
direct violation of the existing compact. That
Russia, without the slightest justification, has
thrust herself into this predicament, is transparent
to the eyes and understanding of collected Europe;
nor can the hypocritical plausibilities of the Czar,
communicated through his pliant mouth-piece,
Count Nesselrode, impose upon the shallowest
understanding, or gain for him a single advocate

in the course which besotted ambition or blind fanaticism is prompting him to follow.

Turkey has made vast strides during the fourteen years of peace which she has been permitted to enjoy. Perhaps no country in Europe has advanced so rapidly. Her navy is respectable, her army well-disciplined and numerous; her old prejudices are giving way to the influence of education and increasing intercourse with other nations; her resources have multiplied, her commerce has increased; her religious toleration extends to the utmost limits which Mohammedanism allows; her Christian subjects are satisfied with their condition and not desirous of change; schools of instruction in literature, science, and arts, are established in all her provinces; her domestic legislation is impartially administered, nor is there any despotic government under which the vice of corruption is so little encouraged. Turkey has, in fact, astonished both her friends and enemies by her marvellous resuscitation, which those who spoke and wrote of her as "a galvanized corpse," are now very slow to believe, notwithstanding her manly efforts in self-defence, and single-handed, since the last invasion of the Principalities. But although Russia during these fourteen years has been compelled to abstain from declared hostility, she has propagated her subverting doctrines through a thousand insidious channels, and has instilled them into the inmost arteries of the Turkish empire. It is indeed difficult to comprehend how reform can have advanced so rapidly, and national strength have been enabled to consolidate itself, in despite of these paralyzing checks. On this important topic, the author of "The Frontier Lands of the Christian and the Turk," (an evidence whose value is extensively admitted,) has put on record some observations which may be relied on as conveying the truth, and may be studied with advantage by those blind diplomatists who still believe, or affect to put faith, in the honesty of a Russian manifesto. He says—"The agent of the Danish company at Widdin received me with great politeness, and after some conversation on the days of sailing, he treated me to a narrative of the last insurrection, with all its circumstances; but his hostility to the Turks was so evident in everything he said, that I could not hear it without considerable distrust. This steamboat agent is also the Vice-consul of Austria. Russia has her secret emissaries; but England has no one to watch the intrigues of these two powers in this quarter, which is so important to Turkey, and consequently interesting to Great

Britain. A mistaken system of economy may sometimes prove prejudicial to the general policy of a cabinet which thus deprives itself, from the most laudable motives no doubt, of information which might guide it in critical circumstances. Here was an insurrection, for instance, which Russia and Austria made much of, and England possessed no means of gaining accurate intelligence about it. All the trade of Upper Bulgaria comes to Widdin; Ionian subjects are much engaged in it, as well as in the general navigation of the Danube, for which this town is one of the principal stations, and for want of a British consular flag to protect them they seek patronage from Austria; and not only do these evils arise from a wish to save a few hundreds per annum, but the general tendency of one of the richest and most influential provinces in European Turkey is consequently ignored by our government, which should know it and guide it also; for I am free to say that in Downing Street there is not the most remote idea of the existence of a comprehensive establishment for the Russianizing of Bulgaria; and yet the Foreign Office can well appreciate the great importance of such a fact. It is by education that this deep-laid scheme is in a course of active execution; no less than twenty-one schools have been instituted of late in the different towns for this purpose; the teachers have all come from Kiew in Russia. Hatred to the Sultan and attachment to the Czar, are assiduously taught; and their catechism in the Sclavonian tongue, which was translated to me, is more practical than religious, while it openly alludes to the incorporation of Bulgaria in the Russian Empire. Besides this, the *propaganda* of the Pan-Sclavonian Hetairia, and the agency of this political interest, opposed to those of Turkey, are efficiently represented by skilful apostles in Bulgaria."

The insurrectionary movements in the different provinces of the Ottoman empire, instead of being produced by Turkish oppression, which has no existence, are invariably fomented by Russian intrigues, which never slumber, and are always on the alert to take advantage of any colourable pretext that may occur. The peasants of Bulgaria, who have been subject to the Turks for five hundred years, are infinitely better off in every respect, in diet, clothing, lodging, and in the produce derived from their agricultural labour, than any of the Sclavonic race, be they of what creed they may, who are doomed to drag on their existence under the iron domination of Russia. The Sultan is accused of intolerance, whereas it is his very tolerant and unsuspecting system of government which gives the opportunity to the secret agents of Russia, of sowing the seeds of discontent amongst the two great sections of his subjects; and of urging them into rebellion, when all are disposed to be happy, loyal, and industrious. The catechism taught in the schools of Bulgaria, by these Muscovite Jesuits, is undoubtedly a duplicate of the scriptural doctrine instilled into the rising generation of Poland, under terror of the knout; and by order of the government. The following extract* may serve as a sample of the whole.

" Qu. 1.—How is the authority of the Emperor to be considered in reference to the spirit of Christianity?

" Ans.—As proceeding immediately from God.

" Qu. 17.—What are the supernaturally revealed motives for this worship of the Emperor?

" Ans.—The supernaturally revealed motives are: that the Emperor is the vicegerent and minister of God, to execute the divine commands; and consequently disobedience to the Emperor is identified with disobedience to God himself; that God will reward us in the world, for the worship and obedience we render the Emperor,

* Quoted in the "Progress and Present Position of Russia in the East."

and punish us severely to all eternity, should we disobey or neglect to worship him. Moreover, God commands us to love and obey from the inmost recesses of the heart, every authority, and particularly the Emperor; not from worldly considerations, but from apprehensions of the final judgment."

Such bold blasphemy has never been approached since the days of pagan darkness, when kings and conquerors voted themselves into the synod of Olympus, decreed their own immortality, and issued edicts announcing their special deification.

And this precious document emanates from the authority of a man, who provokes war " in the name of the Most Holy Trinity," who, with religion on his tongue, remorseless ambition at his heart, and a destroying sword in his hand, imagines himself a semi-deity upon earth, the delegated instrument of omnipotence, and the destined uprooter of the faith of Islam, which with all its errors, is nearer to a reflection of the truth, than his unmitigated bigotry.

The believers in Russian moderation and good faith, if any yet exist, will, we should think, be sufficiently converted by the startling documents which were lately laid before the Houses of Parliament, and have been copied at full length into the public papers. The Emperor Nicholas does not here, as Benedict says of Claudio, turn ortho-grapher, and cook his words into a fantastical banquet, but he speaks plainly and to the purpose, without circumlocution or disguise. As far back as 1844, when he did us the honour of a visit, he anticipated the immediate dissolution of the Turkish empire, and proposed to the English government to divide the inheritance of the dying patient they were mutually pledged to keep in health as long as they could. But Turkey pos-sesses as many lives as a cat, and has rallied several times when given over by the physicians. Finding his overture ill received, the Czar changes his tactics, and says, "let us wait the course of events, and in the meantime forbear to press the Porte by overbearing demands, supported in a manner humiliating to its dignity and independence!" He then proceeds to put in practise the course he repudiates, as we have seen a bailiff in a barrack square brought under a pump, when particular orders were given to take great care of him.

In 1853, the Czar's patience is exhausted, for the Sultan is not yet *in articulo mortis*. He and his empire are as tenacious of life as the Reverend Mr. Blandy, under the homæopathic doses of his affectionate daughter. The Muscovite Machi-avelli again presses the English government. "We have here," says he, "on our hands, a sick man—

a very sick man; one of these days we shall see him slip through our fingers suddenly, before we have disposed of his property, and then others will expect a share : let us be beforehand with them. If you and I agree, a fig for the rest—the treaties of 1840 and 1841 may go into the fire as so much waste paper. Austria cannot move but by my bidding; Prussia I despise; and France I defy. If France dares to despatch an army to the East, I will send it back quicker than it came. Constantinople shall remain provisionally under my protection until I take it to myself—I will incorporate with my own empire, Wallachia, Moldavia, Bulgaria, and Servia, while you shall take possession of Egypt and Candia. My territory I admit is too large already, and my power suspicious as well as dangerous to my neighbours : but notwithstanding, I must have a little addition to both, with which I shall be contented—for the present." This is the sum and substance, the condensed epitome of a long preamble; and, as Lord Ogleby says : "If this isn't plain the devil's in it." Comment on such unparalleled effrontery and double dealing is superfluous. The tone of insolence adopted towards France is too extravagant to excite anything but a smile. A great nation, conscious of its strength, may indulge in contempt, where anger would be undignified. Prussia is wholly passed over as a petty German principality, which can scarcely be discovered on the map without spectacles; while Austria is treated as a dependent province. "The policy of Russia and of Austria," says the dictator, "is one and the same. When I speak of the one country, I mean the other. Austria shall not walk, nor talk, nor move, nor think but as I please." Unless Austria is as false as himself, a very short time will show how far he has overrated his influence.

The correspondence now published, is a manifesto to the world, which will be translated into many languages and perused by millions of intelligent readers. It will furnish valuable material to the future historian, who, while he dilates with honest indignation on the selfish hypocrisy of the Czar, will record with corresponding eulogy the conduct of the English ministers, who were too clear-sighted to be cajoled, too honourable to be tempted, and who disentangled themselves from a labyrinth of "delicate" negotiation, without losing their own credit, or compromising the character and moral ascendency of the sovereign and nation they represented.

The Russian Emperor affects the gallant bearing of Francis the First, and says: "Trust me on the honour of a gentleman, if you doubt my assurance as a monarch. I propose to you great advantages, why will you not accept them frankly?" We reply with Capys the Trojan, when he hurled his javelin against the wooden horse: *"Timeo Danaos et dona ferentes,"*—we are on our guard against a Greek, particular when he proffers kindness.

The Emperor Nicholas is approaching sixty years of age, and has entered on the twenty-ninth of his reign, a long occupation of the throne, in a country where sovereigns are seldom suffered to exhale in the course of nature. If he ever ponders over the annals of his house, he must observe that few of his predecessors have enjoyed such a protracted exercise of absolute power. The ambition which he restrained in manhood he reserves as a solace for his decline. There is a strong similarity between ambition and avarice, although the first has been generally attributed as a quality of great minds, the latter of base ones. Both proceed from a desire of having what we have not, and can very well do without. Some peace advocates have persuaded themselves, that the Czar intends only to retain permanent possession of the Principalities; and has no design of marching on Constantinople, or of subverting the Turkish empire. It has been also thought that if the French and English fleets had moved into the Black Sea on his first threat of crossing the Pruth, in case his demands were rejected by the Porte, that he would not then have carried his threat into execution. The latter opinion can never now be more than conjectural; the former will soon be brought to issue. In the meanwhile Turkey has gained time, confidence, and powerful allies. Her enemy is either "infirm of purpose," or has miscalculated his means of carrying that purpose into effect.

The western nations having been drawn into the war most unwillingly, nothing now remains but to put forth all their strength, and to make the struggle, short, sharp, and decisive. Europe cannot bear a protracted fever of excitement, nor submit to perpetual irritations of alarm; neither can the progress of civilized improvement again be checked by an unprovoked ebullition of barbarism. It matters little whether a dangerous madman be demented by hereditary insanity, superstitious fanaticism, or vulgar drunkenness. In either case he becomes a social pestilence which requires immediate removal. France and England have well remembered the advice of Polonius to Laertes, "beware of entrance to a quarrel," but "being in," we may be well assured they will so bear themselves, that the opposer will rue the hour when he provoked the coalition, which bids fair to drive him back to his deserts, and to keep his hordes within their natural barriers, from whence they ought never

to have been encouraged to emerge. The peace
of Europe has trembled in the balance, ever since
Cossacks of the Don and Bashkir Tartars found
themselves lounging along the boulevards of Paris,
and gloating over the refined luxuries of the
Palais Royal. There was prospective danger in
stimulating the appetite of the wolf, by a glimpse
of the prey he was not permitted to devour.

Out of evil springs good; and but for the blind
obstinacy of the Russian autocrat, the present
cordial co-operation between France and England
might never have taken place. The rivalry of
the two great nations in friendship, will surpass
their former efforts when arrayed against each
other in enmity. The leading questions that
present themselves are, which are the most
obvious points to strike against, and what are the
eligible modes of attack. We need not doubt
that these considerations will be well weighed,
and that ample means will be directed by adequate
judgment. The warning of our great departed
chief has been remembered; and all the preparations indicate that England is not now going to
fritter away strength in " a little war."

In 1836, Marshal Marmont published his views
on the defence of Turkey, supposing the Ottoman
Empire to be, as it now is, threatened by Russia
from the Black Sea and the Danubian Princi-

palities. This work assumes a revived interest
at the present crisis. It was well translated by
Colonel Sir Frederick Smith, of the Engineers,
who has added original observations of his own,
which considerably increase its value. These
notes bear directly on the existing aspect of
affairs, and the *entente cordiale* so happily established between France and England. We need
scarcely remind our readers, that Marmont,
although he shared the fate of greater generals
than himself when he encountered a mighty
master in the art of war, was nevertheless reputed
to be a skilful strategist: he had been trained as
an artillery officer by a regular education, and
had practically studied, in all its degrees, the
science of attack and defence. He was not particularly distinguished by readiness in handling
troops on a field of battle. In that prominent
quality, Moreau, Massena, Ney, and Soult, were
infinitely his superiors. He could arrange a plan
of campaign, although he wanted the inspiration
which seized and grappled with a lucky accident.
His manœuvres, previous to Salamanca, were
showy and imposing; but, in the battle itself,
he made a false step, and was fixed on the
instant, as by a thunderbolt. He was unfortunate in the Peninsula in 1812, unfortunate at
Montmartre in 1814, and, if possible, even more

unfortunate for Charles the Tenth, at Paris, in 1830.

An impression of ill-luck attaches to his memory, and has dimmed his reputation; but his opinions on the "trade of war" are able and deserving of respect.   He points to Adrianople as the central position from whence Turkey is to be defended, supposing the line of the Balkan to be forced or turned.   Portugal and Torres Vedras attest that a country is not conquered, although the frontier is no longer tenable.   But the French marshal's conclusions are all based on the supposition that Russia will take the initiative with her Black Sea fleet, as well as with her army in the Principalities; and will forestall England or France, or both, in the passage of the Bosphorus and the command of the Dardanelles. Here is evidently the vulnerable flank of Constantinople; and had the Russian emperor, at the same moment when he crossed the Pruth and poured his legions into Moldavia and Wallachia, sent his fleet, with twenty thousand picked troops on board, straight down to the eastern capital, it would be difficult to gainsay that he might have produced a revolution in Turkey, and have realized his long-meditated projects by the suddenness of the blow.   The Turkish fleet, unaided, could have offered no adequate resistance.   The breach of faith, the violation of existing treaties, was already committed; a second step, following the first, would have been counted as a trifling aggravation. From weakness of head, and not from any wavering of the heart or scruples of conscience, he has let this opportunity slip through his fingers, which he can never retrieve. He could searcely have sacrificed more character by throwing off the mask at once, and recklessly playing the part of Attila or Gengis, than by halting half-way, and having recourse to the shuffling chicanery of Castruccio Castrucani. Collected Europe has fathomed his duplicity, and traced it to its source. His half-measures are the result of deficiency in executive power, rather than the consequences of a change of inclination. The giant of brass has betrayed the feet of clay.

Russia, by strict engagement and a recorded treaty, to which the other powers are parties, is bound to keep clear the Sulina mouth of the Danube, so that there are always sixteen feet of water clear above the bar. This depth has been suffered, by studied and intentional neglect, to diminish to nine, and will rapidly become less with every succeeding year under such faithless guardianship. The Danube is not a Russian stream; it flows through no Russian territory, and the Russians ought never to have been permitted to exercise the power of obstructing its mouths. Let it be remembered, that while this important care, under an earlier convention, was confided to Turkey, the prescribed conditions were most punctiliously fulfilled. No power in the European confederacy is more scrupulous in the observance of treaties than the Ottoman Porte. Russia, too, imposes a code of uncalled-for sanitary restrictions, equally expensive and harassing, which clog the wheels of commerce, and render them almost stationary. The object is to throw, if possible, the whole trade of the Danube into her own hands; or, failing this, to obstruct it altogether, and to close up what ought to be an open river. The two other outlets of St. George and Kilia are also within the line of the Russian boundary.

England, France, and more especially Austria and Turkey, are vitally interested in preventing this destructive monopoly of a river which, by the Treaty of Vienna, in 1815, was declared a common highway for the whole world. Turkey has long felt and groaned under the heavy grievance; but Austria, blind to her own interest, or silenced by dependence and gratitude, aids and abets in a course of selfish policy which she ought to be the first to oppose.

The exports of corn from Odessa supply a most

important source of Russian revenue. As these exports rise and fall, the commercial pulse of the southern provinces quickens, or stagnates. If Russia can block out the produce of Sclavonia, the Bannat, Bosnia, Servia, Wallachia, and Bulgaria, or drive it northward into her own ports, before it can find vent to the Mediterranean and Western Europe, through the Bosphorus and Dardanelles, her own returns will augment in the same proportion that those of the other countries deteriorate. The power that commands the Black Sea, commands, at the same time, the Danube, with all its numerous arteries teeming with life and incalculable wealth.

It is unsafe to leave this common property a moment longer in the hands of a trustee who has betrayed his duty. The interests of Europe call for an immediate transfer. In order to put an end to the baleful influence which has prevailed too long, and to establish an advanced citadel, a central post, as a guarantee for the observance of treaties, the CRIMEA must be wrested from the wholesale plunderers who obtained this valuable territory under false pretences. The Black Sea controls the Danube, and the Crimea governs the Black Sea. France and England seek no territorial acquisitions for themselves. The Emperor Napoleon has emphatically said,

"The days of conquest are passed away for ever;" but restitution is very different from conquest, and restitution is necessary for the establishment of a just balance, for the future security of the Sultan, and as a first instalment for the massacre of Sinope.

The inhabitants of the Crimea, Tartar in origin, and but little changed since they passed under the dominion of Russia, have no feelings in unison with their present rulers, and would gladly hail the hour of deliverance. This peninsula, the ancient Taurica Chersonesus, barren and flat towards the north, is in the southern portion one of the most beautiful districts in the world, rich in fertility and natural resources. The valleys are astonishingly productive, and the climate extremely mild, from the exclusion of those violent winds by which the northern division is frequently incommoded. The lower hills extending from Caffa to the eastern extremity, are principally used in gardening, and produce a great variety of excellent fruit. The principal articles of export are corn, salt, honey, female slaves brought from Circassia, wax, butter, horses, hides, and furs, especially the Tauric lambskins, which are held in high esteem. Towards the end of the thirteenth century, the Genoese settled in this country, but were expelled by the Crim Tartars in 1474. There are many interesting remains of antiquity, mines, caverns, and objects of natural curiosity. The present population might be quadrupled under good government, with reasonable security for life and property: at present it falls below 300,000. The superficial area of the land is equal to the Morea, and about one-third less than that of the modern kingdom of Greece, without reckoning the islands in the Archipelago. The Isthmus of Perekop, which connects the Crimea with the main-land, is strongly fortified, and extends about four miles and a half across from sea to sea. It would not be difficult to insulate it entirely, and to strengthen the lines so as to render them impregnable. It seems likely that the ancient Taurida was an island when the waters of the Black Sea were also higher than at present, as appears from various historical passages of ancient writers. Pliny, in the fourth book of his Natural History (chapter 26) expresses himself very clearly to this effect.* A full description of the Crimea, its ancient and modern history, races, antiquities, productions, and natural features, is to be found in Pallas's and Clarke's travels. Few countries are more full of noteworthy vestiges, or more

---

* "Sed a Carcinate Taurica incipit, quondam mari circum-fusa; et ipsa, quo nunc jacent campi, deinde vastis attollitur jugis."

deserving of study, independent of the interest with which this locality is now invested by the political citcumstances of the hour. The inhabitants, in a period of internal discord, sought the *protection* of the Empress Catherine, and soon passed under the inevitable yoke which all who have ever been tempted to throw themselves on the tender mercies of Russia are doomed to bear. The southern district of the Crimea, which we háve already named as inviting, has been eulogized by Bishop Heber as an earthly paradise. Dr. Clarke gives a. most animated and heartrending account of the cruelties and wanton butchery perpetrated by Potemkin and Suvaroff during the early occupation, and the misery brought upon a land which, like Poland, had committed no error, and was guilty only of being defenceless. The seaward fortifications of the great Russian naval emporium and arsenal, Sebastopol, are formidable, as far as regards the number of guns and the position of the batteries. Colonel Chesney, no mean authority, is decidedly of opinion that Sebastopol is safe against an attack by the combined fleets· According to a plan just published from a Russian survey of 1836, enlarged by Mr. J. C. Jones, second master of H.M.S. Retribution, there are 722 guns of heavy calibre in forts and batteries, with reckoning the broadsides of the men of-war,

which could all be so placed as to be brought to
bear on the entrance of the harbour. This mouth,
where the Retribution first anchored, is little
more than half a mile in breadth. Marshal Marmont and Mr. Oliphant differ materially in their
estimate of the extent of the fortifications of Sebastopol; and although in the abstract, a military
opinion is to be preferred on a purely military
point, the English traveller having visited the
place very recently, while the inspection of the
French Marshal dates back nearly twenty years,
we must compare the two accounts *cæteris paribus*,
and judge accordingly.

Mr. Oliphant says: " Nothing can be more formidable than the appearance of Sebastopol from
the seaward. Upon a future occasion we visited
it in a steamer, and found that at one point we
were commanded by twelve hundred pieces of
artillery; fortunately for a hostile fleet, we afterwards heard that these could not be discharged
without bringing down the rotten batteries upon
which they are placed, and which are so badly
constructed, that they look as if they had been
run up by contract. Four of the forts consist of
three tiers of batteries. We were, of course, unable to take a very general survey of these celebrated fortifications, and therefore cannot vouch
for the truth of the assertion, that the rooms in

which the guns are worked, are so narrow and ill
ventilated, that the artillery-men would be inevi-
tably stifled in the attempt to discharge their
guns and their duty; but of one fact there was
no doubt, that however well fortified may be the
approaches to Sebastopol by sea, there is nothing
whatever to prevent any number of troops landing
a few miles to the south of the town, in one of the
six convenient bays with which the coast, as far as
Cape Kherson, is indented, and marching down the
main street (provided they are strong enough to
defeat any military force that might be opposed
to them in the open field), sack the town, and
burn the fleet."

It would be neither safe nor wise to act on the
supposed insufficiency of the batteries of Sebastopol. The experiment might end in the disa-
greeable result of "catching a Tartar." There is
not the slightest occasion to be in a hurry, to
damage our ships or to run them heedlessly against
stone walls. A few weeks will place at our dis-
posal ample means to invest Sebastopol by land,
when four-and-twenty hours will settle the business.

Many signal instances may be appealed to
in which ships have engaged and silenced formidable batteries ; as at Copenhagen, Algiers, Acre,
and St. Juan de Ulloa. But history presents us

with as many more, in which they have either
failed or been crippled to a ruinous extent.

At Santa Cruz, in Teneriffe, on the 20th April,
1657, Admiral Blake ran in and destroyed a fleet
of sixteen Spanish men-of-war, moored under the
protection of the castle and batteries. The place
was so strong, that all who knew it wondered
how any man, in his sober senses, could undertake such a desperate enterprise. Had not the
wind changed exactly at the critical moment,
and enabled him to carry his ships back again
when the work was done, all the skill and courage
in the world would have been insufficient to get
him out of the scrape. His great victory would
have ended in a disaster more calamitous than
that which befel Nelson in his unsuccessful attack
on the same place, one hundred and forty years
later.

At Carthagena (in South America) in 1740,
Admiral Vernon was so roughly handled, that
although he took several of the forts, he abandoned the attempt, and with difficulty saved his
disabled ships. On the great combined attack
against the British garrison by the Spanish
floating batteries and fleet (13th September,
1782) at Gibraltar, the efficacy of stone-walls,
when manned by resolute gunners, was most
triumphantly exhibited.

Another remarkable illustration, on a small scale, occurred to that hare-brained warrior, Sir Sidney Smith, when cruizing on the coast of Naples in 1806, which proved, that although he revelled in the smell of gunpowder, and was ever full of fight to overflowing, he sometimes lacked the better part of valour—discretion; and was not always, as Lord Randolph says of Norval, "as wise as brave." In the Pompée, an eighty-gun ship, he ran close in-shore at Point Licosa, and gave battle to an old round tower, with a single traversing-gun mounted on the top. After blazing away broadside after broadside without effect, until he had lost a lieutenant, two midshipmen, eight seamen killed, and thirty-four wounded, he hauled off, and concluded as he ought to have begun, by manning the boats, which pulled in rapidly, and landed the crews with a party of marines, who got round behind; whereupon the bold defender of the tower hoisted the white flag and surrendered, saying that he was very sorry for what had happened, which entirely arose from the mistake of not sending him a civil summons before the firing commenced.

English sailors can do anything; and, in all human probability, would force their way into the inner harbour of Sebastopol, and destroy the Russian fleet at anchor; but two or three ships might be sunk, others disabled, and many valuable lives would certainly be thrown away in fighting against chances which we should thus volunteer to throw into the opposite scale. Twenty thousand men landed at Balaclava, within a short march, attended by a train of artillery and a sufficient supply of siege implements, not forgetting a few rockets (while the fleet blockades the mouth of the harbour), would reduce the business to a calculation of hours, without sending our brave tars to run the gauntlet through an enfilade of batteries, before they can get within arm's length of enemies, who will think many times before they dare to face them in open combat. The most satisfactory triumph is that which achieves the greatest result with the smallest amount of loss. The Crimea can be taken in the regular way; and once in our possession, the teeth of Russia are effectually drawn. We are not now pushed for time, but our foe is. Every hour adds to the strength of the allies and the confidence of Turkey. If the Russian armies in Wallachia and Moldavia cannot cross the Danube in force, and strike an important blow before the French and English troops arrive, what is there before them but a disastrous retreat immediately after? Neither is their position on the Asiatic side likely to improve by delay. Circassia is panting to retaliate on her invaders, and Georgia is ready to assist. The passing hours are worth their weight in gold to Russia, yet they glide on and she does nothing. Again, we repeat, she is colossal in an ukase, gigantic in a bulletin, but of very ordinary dimensions in an actual campaign, when resolutely opposed. What has she gained in nine months against Turkey, fighting alone, and without the forces of France and England, now steaming rapidly to the rescue? Nothing beyond the ignominy of Sinope, and the undisguised wishes of the whole world for her speedy humiliation. The Turks have held their ground, beaten them in every encounter, and the frowning lines of Kalafat are still unassailed. Potemkin issued his orders to Suvaroff, to take Ismail at any cost — and he did it; Nicholas has said the same to Gortchakoff with regard to Kalafat—and he has not done it. The memory of Suvaroff will not supply his rare talent and unconquerable daring.

It is still believed by many that the Russian Emperor will succumb at the twelfth hour, and offer to negotiate before he tries the last chance of battle. If his madness be the fanaticism of what he fancies to be a religious obligation, there is no hope of this; but circumstances may control even a Russian autocrat, and bend him to submission, without his being allowed a voice in the matter. The northern confederacy of 1801 was broken up by the violent catastrophe we have already touched upon, and which assuredly the son of Paul has not forgotten. Under any contingency, it is devoutly to be hoped that while we disclaim conquest, we should remain deaf as adders to compromise or treaty, without ample indemnity for the past and certain security for the future. The snake must be killed, not scotch'd. We have ample experience to refer to, showing how often we have suffered from ill-timed generosity, and given up all, when all was in our power. Spare your enemy when he asks for quarter, but take from him the means of being mischievous a second time.

The English people are quite reconciled to a temporary visitation of the augmented income tax, and will pay it cheerfully; but the prospect of a permanent one, or a protracted contest, will make them close up their breeches-pockets, and betake themselves to their old trade of grumbling. Russia not only fights with the open weapons of war, but uses the secret agencies of intrigue in a thousand ramifications. Her emissaries are at work in Paris and in London at this moment. They are in the ports of the United States, endeavouring to promote the equipment of American privateers under the Russian flag.

They are in Greece, in Albania, in Bosnia, in Servia, in Bulgaria, in Roumelia. They are in Constantinople, and are possibly in the Sultan's cabinet. They are in the fortresses, the camps, the cities, the villages, the mountains, and the plains. Money will buy treason everywhere, and money will not be spared as long as it lasts. Let King Otho take good care that he is not implicated. He too is under protection, but the powers that made, can unmake, if they see cause. His rickety kingdom stands on a weak foundation, and is to all intents and purposes, a moral and political failure; a thorn in the side of Turkey, an excrescence without wholesome vitality; a mere Russian outpost, and a convenient focus for Russian intrigue. The establishment of that mock independence was a philanthropical blunder, a yielding-up of sound policy to classical recollections, a school-boy tenderness for the memories of Solon and Lycurgus, of Pericles and Leonidas;—a practical mistake, as fatal as was the " untoward event of Navarino." What has Greece yet done, collectively or individually, to prove herself worthy of the attempt at regenerating a people who will not co-operate in regenerating themselves? They still exhibit the Pyrrhic dance, the ancient costume, the language, and the proverbial duplicity; but of the patriotic virtue, the hardy valour which won Salamis and consecrated Thermopylæ, which scattered the hosts of Xerxes and carried the Ten Thousand over six hundred leagues through countdangers, from Assyria to the courts of Ionia, they retain nothing save the imperishable records of Herodotus, Thucydides, and Xenophon.

A quarter of a century ago, Philhellenism was a raging epidemic in England. The genius and early death of Lord Byron enveloped the struggle for Grecian freedom with a halo of glory and expectation. Time the purifier has sobered enthusiasm down to reality, and dissipated the dreams of romance. A country has much to learn in the common rudiments of moral instruction, of which a conscientious traveller writes :* "The ministry allege that even the very chairs and tables in the ministerial hotels are not safe; the Queen declines going to the theatre, because the furniture of her box was stolen; and there are villages in Acarnania where one day in the year is *consecrated* to theft."

The doubt so long entertained that Austria would exert or side with Russia, may now be looked upon as removed by her late positive declaration. Her geographical position gives her

* The Rev. H. Christmas's "Shores and Islands of the Mediterranean."

an importance beyond her actual strength, and her course has been wisely chosen with a view to her own future security. The King of Prussia is still hesitating, his people are dissatisfied, and their position is critical. He is attached to the Emperor of Russia by personal intimacy, congenial habits, and matrimonial alliance; but states acknowledge no private ties, although sovereigns are frequently biassed by them. Prussia is the smallest of the great powers. Her territory is compact, her coast-line well defined, her revenue sufficient, her army numerous and of first-rate quality; but her population does not exceed sixteen millions, and she lies within reach of the devouring Maelstrom, which swallows up all that comes within its vortex. But Prussia, as a leading member of the German confederacy, has a double interest in opposing a barrier to the encroachments of her dangerous neighbour, and should make common cause with Sweden and Denmark, in the event of an attempt to coerce her decision.

With a view to repelling the aggressions of Russia, and to prevent their recurrence in future, our efforts naturally direct themselves to the East and the Black Sea. For the just retaliation which she has loudly demanded, we turn towards the North and the Baltic. In the first quarter,

Russia may strike with a chance of success, if she is prompt and powerful; in the latter, she can only look for heavy blows without the probability of a return. It may be taken for granted that her fleets will avoid an action with ours in the open sea. If they are rash enough to risk one, they are not likely to return to the harbours from whence they sailed. Their naval qualities have never yet been proved, except in combat with the Turks, and once in an action with a very superior force against the Swedes. Their experience is principally confined to waters which are not navigable during half the year; long voyages round the world, doubling Cape Horn and the Cape of Good Hope, are beyond the limits of their ordinary practice. Lord Nelson had not a very exalted opinion of Russian seamanship. He studied the characteristics of every enemy he was likely to encounter, as minutely as a pilot examines his charts, or a steersman watches the motion of the compass. He used to say, " close with a Frenchman or a Spaniard, but dodge a Russian." His meaning was, that, being inexpert in the handling of ships, complicated movements would confound and place them at the mercy of a more active opponent. Steam will entirely change the features of naval warfare, and must leave the chances of battle more dependent on the skill of the admiral, who, through such a controlling engine, wields a power which renders him independent of winds, calms, or currents. The consequences of this novel agency have as yet only been calculated on surmise; no opportunity has occurred of testing them by experiment. Formerly, as the great authority named above observed, when delivering instructions to his officers, " no captain of a British man-of-war could be far wrong, who lays his ship close alongside his enemy." But steam, and above all the screw propeller, enables him now to come into action exactly after the manner and in the position chosen by himself. If he is out-manœuvred, the fault is entirely his own. Battles will be shorter and more decisive than they used to be, and the comparative loss on either side will depend in a much greater degree on the ability of the respective commanders, whose responsibility is increased in a similar proportion. A close-broadside combat between two vessels carrying such a tremendous weight of metal as our modern three-deckers, could not possibly last for many minutes without the certain annihilation of both.

The destruction of the arsenal and ships at Cronstadt might possibly be accomplished by the combined attack of a naval and military expedition, in the face of any defensive preparations. We are not prepared to say whether this advantage would not be too dearly purchased by the loss of lives, and probable damage to our vessels, at which sacrifice the result would be obtained. The entire command of the Baltic, which our naval superiority will ensure, as it has already done of the Euxine, will as effectually cripple the profitable strength of Russia, as the mere destruction of ships which she is unable to use. Her fleet becomes a nominal display when it cannot liberate her commerce, or open the only mouth through which that commerce permeates into the ordinary channels. If this outlet is permanently sealed up by the cruisers of France and England, the unwieldy empire becomes an inert, putrescent body, deprived of the limbs which give it life and healthy action. Much of the influence of Russia is derived from the opinion which has been pertinaciously disseminated of her invincible strength, her myriads of soldiers, and her unbounded resources; an opinion that will rapidly subside if the two former are exhausted, and the springs of the latter dried up, There can be no doubt that the united power of France and England can produce this revolution, which will teach the Emperor of Russia a convincing lesson, that enormous masses of men, moved like machines, must stop when they reach the sea-shore, and are not the only elements of national strength.

Next to Poland, there is no country which has been so ill-treated as Finland, and none to which Russia has so little claim. It was treacherously won, and has been cruelly trampled on. The inhabitants remember their long incorporation with Sweden, the happiness they enjoyed under her rule, the military reputation which they materially assisted her to acquire, and the commerce which formerly flowed into their ports. They participated in the glories of Leipzig, Lutzen, and Narva, and recruited the ranks of Gustavus Adolphus and Charles the Twelfth, with brave and loyal soldiers. They are the only real mariners the Russians can find to man their ships, and are compelled to fight reluctantly under the claws of the eagle, while their eyes are turned with the sickness of hope deferred to the Swedish cross. They would rise to a man and do battle to the death, to escape from the *protection* of Russia, and return back to their ancient nationality.

When Buxhowden, in 1808, under the orders of the Emperor Alexander, wrested Finland from Sweden, he issued a proclamation, expressing the deep regret of his master that he was compelled to invade a peaceful country for the purpose of obtaining a guarantee that the King of Sweden would submit to whatever terms he might please to dictate. At the same time he promised not to interfere with their internal legislation, to leave them the full exercise of their laws, statutes, and customs, and to pay and feed his troops entirely at his own expense. A few months later, the Swedish monarch addressed a letter to the Emperor of Russia, which speaks eloquently for the manner in which this proclamation was observed. "Honour and humanity," he says, "require me to make strong representations against the innumerable horrors and vexations which the Russian armies have permitted themselves in Swedish Finland. The blood of the innocent victims calls for vengeance upon those who authorized such cruelties. Can it be made a crime in my Finnish subjects not to have wished to let themselves be seduced by promises which are as fallacious as the principles on which they are founded are erroneous? Is it worthy of a sovereign to make it in them a crime? I conjure your Imperial Majesty to put an end to the calamities and the horrors of a war which ought to call down on your person and your empire the malediction of Divine Providence." It must be remembered that this remonstrance was called forth long after resistance in the field had ceased, and Sweden had bowed under the loss of the province she was too feeble to retain.

Russian rule is more detested in Finland than in any other appanage of the empire. Sweden has been unjustly plundered of a larger territory than she has been suffered to retain, and weakened down to a third-rate power, when sound policy dictated her restoration to the rank she formerly maintained. Russia at present controls the Baltic with overwhelming superiority. If Finland were restored to Sweden, the balance would be re-established, and a better security obtained for the future than the capture of a few ships, which are easily replaced, or the destruction of dockyards and fortresses, which rise rapidly from their ruins. The point is one deserving of profound consideration, and the consequences involved are of the first importance. It would be unjust to encourage the Finlanders to take up arms on a delusive prospect, unless it was quite determined to support them to the end, and enforce their emancipation.

And now the formalities of the tournament are complete, the knights are in the lists, with vizors closed and lances in rest. The marshal of the field has proclaimed the signal, " Laissez aller!" and the combatants are eager to engage. In a few weeks, perhaps days, the thunder of artillery will re-echo from the shores of the Baltic and the Black Sea. The issue is in the hand of heaven, and no human intelligence can say whether the impending conflict will be long or short, or how the fluctuating tide of success may direct its course. France and England have done all that is consistent with the duties of the two foremost nations of the globe to preserve peace, as long as peace was compatible with safety and existing treaties. Compelled at last to have recourse to the *ratio ultima regum,* the final arbitrement of bullet and bayonet, we enter into the struggle with a conviction that arms were never appealed to in a sounder cause, and with a prestige of victory, grounded on the extent of the provocation.

War having once commenced, two courses are open to the enemy; a vigorous attack, or a protracted defence. He may push boldly on, and attempt to force his way to Constantinople, in despite of rivers, frontier fortresses, mountain passes, and opposing armies; or he may retire, like a tortoise, within his shell, and wait in defiance of reprisal. If he adopts the former plan the chances in our favour are manifestly increased; if he selects the latter, and pursues the Fabian system of delay, he may harass and worry the allies until some unforeseen accident affords him an opening; but to do this he must possess interminable supplies of treasure; his nobles must

second him with enthusiastic loyalty and submit
to the total suspension of their annual incomes;
the mass of his people must resign themselves to
endure without murmuring the privations that a
long war will entail upon them; and his ranks,
thinned by the sword, disease, and neglect,
must be recruited by miracle, as warriors sprang
in full equipment from the dragon's teeth of
Cadmus.

If he can encounter and surmount all these
impediments, *if* he is prepared to subdue so many
obstacles, the result becomes a very different
calculation; but as honest Touchstone says,
" there is much virtue in an *if;*" and in this case,
the intervening conjunction is more imperatively
indispensable than in the deadly quarrel on the
seventh cause which a bench of magistrates was
unable to adjust.

In venturing these observations, which have
been hastily thrown together, there is no disposition to fall into the error of undervaluing a
formidable opponent. The object is, to bring
down a fabulous Titan to the common standard,
by which he ought in truth to be measured, and
to reduce the inflated spectre of the Hartz Mountains to the reasonable dimensions of an ordinary
bugbear.

Our warriors have departed for their distant

scene of action greeted by the acclamations of assembled thousands, and animated by the presence of the Queen. They need no stirring words, no eloquent appeal, to rouse their inherent valour to exertion, but if we turn to the universal pages of Shakspeare, we find a ready apostrophe, as if composed for the occasion.

> " On ! on ! you noblest English,
> Whose blood is fet from fathers of war-proof !
> Fathers, that like so many Alexanders,
> Have, in these parts, from morn till even fought,
> And sheath'd their swords for lack of argument.
> Be copy now to men of grosser blood,
> And teach them how to war !—and you, good yeomen,
> Whose limbs were made in England, shew us here
> The metal of your pasture; let us swear
> That you are worth your breeding; which I doubt not :
> For there is none of you so mean and base
> That hath not noble lustre in your eyes.
> I see you stand like greyhounds in the slips,
> Straining upon the start.   The game's afoot;
> Follow your spirit; and upon this charge,
> Cry—God for ' Victoria,' England, and St. George !"

THE END.

www.ingramcontent.com/pod-product-compliance
Lightning Source LLC
Chambersburg PA
CBHW030503100426

42813CB00002B/321